Riverine

An Anthology of Hudson Valley Writers

Riverine

An Anthology of Hudson Valley Writers

Edited by
Laurence Carr

Codhill Press
New Paltz, New York

This book is published by Codhill Press,
David Appelbaum, Publisher
First Edition

Printed in the United States of America

Copyright © 2007 by Laurence Carr

ISBN 1-930337-32-0

All rights reserved. No part of this publication protected by this copyright notice may be reproduced or utilized in any form or by any means, electronic, mechanical, including photocopying, recording or by any informational storage and retrieval system, without written permission of the publisher.

Edited by Laurence Carr
Text design by Nan Alderson
Cover design by Tony Davis
Cover Art "Fish Music Part III" (encaustic, oil and collage on wood)
    by Anne Gorrick

Table of Contents

Preface xiv

Acknowledgments xv

Memoir

How Books Changed My Life
    Da Chen 19

Land Ho!
    Laurence Carr 24

Water Babies (published in *Chronogram*)
    Nina Shengold 26

The Perfect House (from *A Place In the Country*, Riverhead Books)
    Laura Shaine Cunningham 30

Sandcastles
    Werner Hengst 39

Short Story

Bones Like Ice
    James P. Othmer 49

The 3-Mile Run
    Anthony Robinson 56

Butterfly Kisses
    Annecy Baez 70

Waterloo
    Jacob Appel 74
Mision San Pablo (published in the *LA Times* Sunday magazine, *West*)
    Steven Lewis 91
Raised Hearts Hailing: The Poems of Francis Eamon Boyle (1874-1900) (published in *Shawangunk Review*)
    William Boyle 99
A Supermarket In Upstate New York: Shadowing Allen Ginsberg
    Barbara Adams 109
Hell On Earth; Heaven Comes; Give Peace A Chance
    Abigail Robin 114

Microfiction and Prose Poem

Stars
    Roberta Allen 125
Anneka (published in *KGB Bar Lit*)
    Roberta Allen 126
String Theory
    Guy Reed 127
Love, Death, Etc. (published in *Eclectica*)
    Howard Good 129
Imagine
    R.E. Rigolino 131
The God of Falling Objects (published in *Sentence: A Journal of Prose Poetics*)
    Christine Boyka Kluge 133
The Woman With The Video Camera
    Bruce Weber 134

Poetry: Hudson Valley Views

Swimming In The Hay Barn (from *Hapax Legomena,* Mellon Poetry Press)
    Barbara Adams 137

The Laws of What Happens (The Lefevre farmhouse, Route 32 North)
    Jacqueline Renée Ahl 139

The Carrion Eaters
    David Appelbaum 142

Rite of Passage
    David Appelbaum 144

Tree Watching
    Brenda Connor-Bey 145

Spring Walks, Mountain Views (published in *Thought*)
    James Finn Cotter 147

Farewell To Summer
    Lynne Digby 155

Designs (from *The Bad Man,* Ye Olde Font Shoppe Press)
    Dennis Doherty 156

Feet (from *The Bad Man,* Ye Olde Font Shoppe Press)
    Dennis Doherty 158

Summer Stage in Winter
    Allen C. Fischer 159

November Kill
    Mala Hoffman 161

Woodstock Mornings
    C.J. Krieger 162

My Hermit (published in *Chronogram*)
    Robert Leaver 163

Carpentry & Gardening
 Phillip Levine 164
Rt. 44/55 at night
 Nadine Lewis 166
Autumn Vintage
 Robert Milby 167
Sister Scarecrows –Cottekill Fire House Community Garden
  (published in *Wisconsin Review*)
 Will Nixon 169
*The Life of the Stag – Catskills (*published in *The Café Review)*
 Will Nixon 171
Heron
 Jo Pitkin 173
Stone House
 Jo Pitkin 175
The Dogs and I Walked Our Woods,
 Gretchen Primack 176
Helping My Parents' Friends Get in Hay
 Matthew J. Spireng 178
Brook
 Matthew J. Spireng 179
Cutting the Oak
 Matthew J. Spireng 180
Ulster Heights, New York
 Christine Lilian Turczyn 181
The Boardwalk (from *In The Salt Marsh*, Knopf)
 Nancy Williard 183

Poetry: Other Realms

Stargazing
   Jay Albrecht 187
Mountain Laurel Children (published in *Stonesthrow Review*)
   Kat Alexander 188
Sometimes A Buddha Poem
   Jerrice Baptiste 190
Tapestry
   Lucia Cherciu 192
Can the Cactus Know the Salamander
   Samuel Claibourne 195
Magnificent
   Suzanne Cleary 197
Goddess Gone Fishing
   Teresa Marta Costa 199
Untenanted (from *Anything You Don't See,* West End Press)
   Enid Dame 200
The Best Education (from SOMBER REUNION, Morning Star
      Press)
   Alec Emerson 203
Villard de Honnecourt
   Staats Fasoldt 205
The Concierge of Hell (published in *Poetry Bay*)
   Howard Good 208
Sorrow's Rooms (published in *The Rose and Thorn*)
   Howard Good 209

Paris: Where All Thursdays Go to Die; after "Black Stone Lying on a White Stone" by César Vallejo (published in *The Cortland Review*)
    Anne Gorrick 210
Mad Evil Times
    Sari Grandstaff 212
Something
    Eamon Grennan 214
Innocence of Things
    Eamon Grennan 216
I Give You Birth (published in *Southern Poetry Review*)
    Carol Graser 218
The Weight of Snow
    Don Haynie 221
Books
    Mikhail Horowitz 223
Morgan
    Mikhail Horowitz 224
Konghuin (a tune for the lyre)
    translated by Heinz Insu Fenkl 225
Grieving for Yin Yao; Wang Wei (701-761 A.D.)
    translated from the Korean by Heinz Insu Fenkl 226
April 1968
    Kate Hymes 227
The Seminar
    Kate Hymes 228
Barrier Canyon Style (published in *The Literary Gazette*)
    Mike Jurkovic 230

Cattle Map (published in *The South Carolina Review*)
    Mike Jurkovic 232

The Skies In Their Mouths
    Christina Boyka Kluge.. 233

Self-Improvement
    Frank LaRonca.. 234

The Ginger Jar
    Sharmagne Leland-St.John 236

Twilight (from *Twilight*, CRS Books)
    Donald Lev.. 239

Scene from a Marriage (from *Yesterday's News*, Red Hill Outloudbooks)
    Donald Lev.. 241

Autistic Superkid (published in *Chronogram*)
    Brian Liston 242

What I Ate
    Valerie Martin 243

You Found Her
    Valerie Martin 244

Grand Central - Passing Through on the Way Home after a Long Day
    Karen Neuberg.. 246

Shooting Star (published in *AGNI*)
    Robert Polito 248

Three Horse Operas (published in *AGNI*)
    Robert Polito 250

Freight Trains
    Marilyn Reynolds.. 251

A Double Life (from *My Night With the Language Thieves*, Ye Olde Font Shoppe Press)
    Tad Richards 254
Conception
    Cheryl A. Rice 258
American Epitaphs
    William Seaton 260
Boca de Tomatlan (published in *The Telluride Watch*)
    William Seaton 262
The persistence of ashes (published in *Front Range Review*)
    Kenneth Salzmann 263
My Mother's Owl Collection (published in *Oxalis*)
    Judith Saunders 265
The Weaver
    Jan Zlotnik Schmidt 267
A Photograph of my Parents in the Catskills, Circa 1937 (published in *Shawangunk Review*)
    Jan Zlotnik Schmidt 269
3 Poems
    Sparrow 271
Ascension (published in *The Webster Review*)
    Margo Stever 272
Conversation with Bertolt Brecht (published in *The New England Review*)
    Margo Stever 274
(excerpt from) THE BORROMEAN ISLANDS; For the Posse
    H. R. Stoneback 276
Untitled
    Christine Lilian Turczyn 282

Elements of Style
    Pauline Uchmanowicz 283
Five-Minute Hamlet
    Pauline Uchmanowicz 284
A Valentine in Green Pastures
    Bob Wright 285
Japanese Coasters
    Robert H. Waugh 286
Popinjay in the Japonica (published in *Shawangunk Review*)
    Sarah Wyman 293

Author Biographies 295

Preface

The Hudson River has flowed through good times and bad, defining our region physically, culturally, socially and intellectually. Over 300 miles, from its Adirondack whisper to its open-throated song to New York City, it created a place unique in history and diversity. A meeting place for the world's people, intermingling while remaining true to their ancestors.

Words flowed here, too, from the earliest times. Both oral and written traditions created a powerful current of stories, journals, personal narratives, and dramas that were drawn from the minds and hearts of those who came to call this river valley home.

Riverine celebrates the words of those authors who breathe the air of this valley, drink its water, eat the harvest from its rich soil and convert these gifts into the gift of words that reflects our individual and collective lives. As long as a healthy Hudson River continues to flow through this valley (and part of our lives must be committed to its good health), the words of its writers will also continue to flow from lips and pens and pencils and keyboards.

An overwhelming number of authors submitted their literary works to *Riverine*. Too many to be included here. The fault of the finite. But to all who did submit and to all who read these pages, you are riverine—relating to or formed by the river. David Appelbaum, publisher of Codhill Press, and I, as editor, thank all of our writers and readers for creating this volume, which we hope will be the source of inspiring journeys.

Laurence Carr, Editor

Acknowledgments

I would like to thank SUNY New Paltz for its ongoing support, especially my colleagues in the English Department and Creative Writing Program.

Special thanks to Nan Alderson, who worked hard on the layout and overall look of this volume and whose advice should always be followed.

Many thanks to my wife, Kay Stuntz, for her belief in the many projects, past, present and future and without whose lasting support there would always be the blank page.

Laurence Carr, Editor

Memoir

How Books Changed My Life

Da Chen

Growing up poor in China during the seventies, I would do anything for a good meal. But I would do even more for books. Books were such a luxury that we often had to hand-copy them to read them. Ironic, then, that I should learn to love reading in the book desert of China.

I wanted to read because I was a storyteller even as a little lad. A storyteller was essential in our village, which didn't have electricity. There were no movies, no malls (not that malls are any substitutes for books), no television. When the sun set, only the moon was supposed to shine in our village. There was a fortuneteller in our village who would sit under a pine tree every summer night, telling and retelling tales of love and hate, war and ghosts that had been handed down for generations. We called him a "Mothman" because he seemed to attract all the moths. He got all the mosquitoes as well, I might add. The entire village would be there after a day's hot labor in the scorching fields. Mothers would be dozing off, breastfeeding their infants, who sucked absentmindedly on their nipples. Fathers would be smoking long pipes, letting the old man's tales wash away their fatigue. I would sit right next to the old man, fanning him, to keep his flow of story going. How I wished I were him.

Soon I became the Mothman of my generation. Every day after school I would gather my followers. We would all climb up the same tree, hanging in the branches like monkeys, and I would tell the stories that I had heard from the real Mothman. My listeners would rub my shoulders, scratch my back, and even light my cigarette to keep my story going.

But the day would come when my stories would go dry and my listeners would stop coming. It was time to hit the bookstore or library. But all libraries were sealed during the Cultural Revolution; Mao forbade us to read any literature except those written by him. And there was no bookstore to speak of; such a little village did not deserve one.

One day a buddy of mine came shouting into my window to tell me that a new bookstore had opened at the edge of our muddy village. We rushed, splashing our way to the store, only to be told that one needed one fen, a Chinese penny, to rent one picture book to read in one sitting. An old convict who had returned from his twenty-year jail term manned the store. He had stolen two big sacks of rare forbidden books from an army library on the eve of his departure — not reformed at all.

We were so poor that we could not even afford one fen. Dad, working day and night, was barely able to feed us with yams. Mom cut all our hair to save money so that we could afford soy sauce. One day, I spotted someone selling his used toothpaste tube to the commune's recycling store. He sold it for a fen, the exact amount needed to rent a book for one good read.

The very next morning, I brushed my teeth five times, each time squeezing a fat worm of toothpaste onto my brush, causing my mother to look at me suspiciously. I mumbled that I intended to heighten my dental care from that day on. She half believed me — my gums were all swollen. Within three days, I used up the entire toothpaste that Mother had bought for fifteen fen, sold the aluminum tube for a fen, and rushed to the store to rent my first book.

The ex-convict wasn't very friendly. He stared at me the whole time I was there, reminding me not to dent the pages, those precious pages, by turning too hastily. The picture book I picked was about a young Frenchman put into a dungeon although he had done no wrong. Within pages, I was sucked into the book so completely that I forgot about the dreary drizzle of that Saturday afternoon. I forgot where I was and I became him, that French boy. I suffered with him in that darkness of hopelessness. Napoleon became my emperor. I flew away from myself, from the little village I was trapped in. The book was *The Count of Monte Cristo*, and it became the inspiration for my recent novel for young readers, *Wandering Warrior*.

Though the book store thrived on the pennies that we village children scraped from whatever means available – selling more used toothpaste tubes, digging rare herbs to sell to the commune's hospital, searching the dusty corners of my father's drawers for those misplaced pennies and collecting dried dog manure – it did not survive long. One day not long after, my buddy screamed hysterically into our window, "The bookstore is on fire!"

We rushed among the un-hurrying water buffalos, loosened from their ploughing duties, toward the village corner where the store stood. The thatched roof of the hut was a ball of fire, spewing a plume of dark smoke into the azure sky. We got so close to the hut that we could feel its heat pinching our skin. The storeowner, usually an abrupt and arrogant man, was reduced to pity. He was sobbing bitterly, trying to run back into the fire to salvage his precious books, and screaming something about wanting to be burned alive with those books. Kind villagers comforted him, pulling him away from his attempts.

The fire soon consumed the entire hut. The ashes were falling from the sky, like dark snowflakes. I reached out my hands, and caught some in my palms. I was sure those ashes contained some of the most magical words that had touched our young hearts, and lifted our souls. But gone were the books, oh, those windows of the world, that had let a glimpse of other worlds into the narrow confines of our village existence. In that one brief second, the ashes were blown away by a quickening sea breeze and our saddened hearts were comforted.

The arsonist was none other than the party secretary of our commune, who had feared that the books were corrupting our young minds. He had wanted to burn the owner as well, and had locked all doors from outside. But the owner managed to escape from an unlocked window.

The communist party chief took the books away from us, but not the seeds that the fine books had sewn in our young hearts. That deprivation didn't stop our thirst for books, it only heightened it. Whenever there was a book in circulation among the villagers, we would rip it apart and hand-copy each chapter, and within days a new book would be made. We roamed other bigger villages looking for sealed libraries to break into, so that we could "borrow" those rotten books, soaked in the muck and overgrown with mold as a result of typhoon storms. Oh, even a moldy book smelled heavenly.

Years later, after I had gotten my law degree from Columbia University and was working in a Wall Street investment bank, I decided to write about my childhood, the childhood of deprivation and dreams. More deprivation breeds more dreams. One of the silent dreams was to write books so that no one could take them away from me. To write books so another village boy somewhere in the dark corners of the earth could subsist upon it, giving him rays of hope and a glimpse of future.

After nine months of writing in my spare time, my first memoir, *Colors of the Mountain*, came to be. With the blessing that could only come from above, the book was won by Random

House's president, Ann Godoff, in an intense five-house auction. It was published to much critical acclaim – some called it a Chinese *Angela's Ashes* – and was a commercial success, scaling the *New York Times* Best Sellers List. A second memoir, *Sounds of the River*, was published two years later, to be followed by my first young adult fiction work, *Wandering Warrior*, which *USA Today* lauded as a "Chinese *Harry Potter*."

Writers write for various reasons, but I write because my heart demands so. There is such a freedom in the simple act of sitting there, holding up my hands, waiting to pound on the computer keyboard, waiting to pour out those words from the tips of my fingers. To compose the melody of life from the fading tapestry of my past. That craving for freedom had come from a deep princely land of my childhood, where books were gold, and a dream was but to hold it in my lap on those dreary Saturday afternoons in that forgotten village, far away near the end of this earth.

Land Ho!

Laurence Carr

For more than twenty-five years, I nurtured a New York City window box of miniature herbs and spindly nondescript flowers, many of which I suspect were volunteers who found shelter through the help of a bird or the wind.

Inside the apartment I kept my love-hate relationship with several potted plants, Mother-In-Law's Tongues, clinging to life despite my neglect interspersed with bouts of over-watering. Green dagger leaves unsheathe, stand defiantly tall, weaken, topple, die- then send their children for revenge. It all seemed so futile, giving over to both blind faith and suicide. An overheated, dark and arid apartment, even for those gardeners with emerald thumbs, is the last stop on the descent to floral hell.

New York City apartment plants. First cousins to those floral displays haunting funeral parlors. And as primped and unnatural as the remains they surround and moments away from mingling their dusts.

But a change of course is bound to happen if you wait long enough. Either you move on or the world will move you. Either way, the next migration comes. Sailing up the Half-Moon Hudson current, I find safe harbor at woodsy Pancake Hollow. The new immigrant disembarks. The hamlet of Highland. I had always wanted to live in a hamlet. Vaguely Shakespearean. A subtle nod to both my wife's Danish and my Scots ancestry.

Upon inspection, the house didn't fall in on itself, or us, so we made the agreement to stay a while. A handshake in the driveway added our names to the list of everyone who'd lived there since 1849.

The original house goes back to 1830. Or 1825. Or 1820. No one knows for sure. Or those who know won't tell. And the original documents kept in imposing drawers in Kingston are fading. Incomplete. But the house stands firm. A story and a half. (I know all about half stories, the ones half-written then left to curl up in cardboard boxes in backs of closets, then finally tossed out with the broken saucers and moldy carpet pads. Oh, yes, I know all about half stories.)

The house was built in fits and starts. And with close inspection, more fits than starts and more starts than finishes. The perfect home for writers, dreamers, procrastinators, mendicants, anarchists, cult leaders.

A place for those who drop out and for those who pray for strength. A place to change from house to home. And with it, a span of land. For a man who lived in a box. A box that had dried out. Worn through. The choice was clear- fall through or move on.

And as I haul the tenth tarp of brush down the hill, I vaguely remember what Scarlett's father said to her. "It's about the land. You'll always have Tara."

I laughed at this in the older days. But now, when I stand very still, and keep very quiet, I faintly hear the voice beneath my feet. I feel it. In my hands, eyes, nose, mouth, inside my shoes and underwear. This land. Entrusted to me. For one short breath of eternity.

Water Babies

Nina Shengold

When my mother's wallet was stolen on a New York City bus, the thing she missed most was a dog-eared black and white snapshot of her only daughter, age two and a half, charging into the waves on a Cape Cod beach. I gazed at that photo so often that its image feels like a memory: uncued, I can conjure the gush of salt surf through my toes and the shrill shrieks of terns swooping over those black and white wavetips.

Water was always our element. Ungainly on land, with frames which are kindly described as "sturdy", my mother and I enter water like emperor penguins, our waddling gait turning fluent and sleek underwater.

The happiest scenes from my childhood all feature water: the summer-long hissing of sprinklers and hoses in tiny back yards, giddy afternoons yelping "Marco!", "Polo!" in the turquoise shallows of a municipal pool. Day camp: bobbing white floats strung on ropes over muddy pond bottoms, sun-crackled Buddy Boards, faded orange life vests shedding kapok like milkweed pods, Grumman canoes. I remember my progress from Minnow to Guppy to Junior Life Saver, and one golden swim meet, the first time my body had ever excelled, winning me a blue ribbon in backstroke. Sometimes on sweltering Sundays my friend Ellen's mother would drive us down to the Jersey shore, kids packed like sardines in the rear-facing seat of a Rambler station wagon. Shrieking with sunburnt, salty-haired glee, we body-surfed over and over, tumbling out of high waves amid sugary, rancid aromas that drifted down from the boardwalk: Salt-Water Taffy and corndogs on sticks, bloated zeppoli frying. Once I miscalculated and came down face first in the undertow, smashing my nose bloody and swallowing lungfuls of seawater. A lifeguard dabbed salve on my bruises and said I was brave. I was eight and in love.

Best of all was the lake. For six summers running, my family rented the same lakefront cabin in upstate New York. I cannot hear the word "August" without picturing my mother's white rubber bathing cap and long, skirted swimsuit, my father's distinctive polar bear crawl as he plowed through that clear, spring-fed water, so cold it brought goosebumps. Every August my brothers and I lived in swimsuits and flip-flops, soaking rump-shaped puddles on picnic benches as we gobbled fistfuls of sandwich and sweet corn before bounding back to the lake. (Our parents pooh-poohed the traditional notion of waiting an hour to prevent stomach cramps.) We dug sanctuaries for red efts and crayfish along the shore, buried dime-store treasures we never recovered, searched for fossils in pieces of shale that my older brother could skim in astonishing arcs, leaving patterns of widening rings.

From our bracing before-breakfast dip to the sunset-gilded last swim of the day, we were creatures of water. We even went swimming in rain. "It takes all the rottenness out," my father would sigh as he floated alongside the dock. When Labor Day came, we lit sparklers and hurled them into dark waves.

Sometimes I think I can chart my life's milestones in bodies of water. As my childhood summers ebbed into the past, there were new currents surging: moonlit idylls in the shimmering, body-warm river behind the summer stock theatre where I was an eager apprentice; a post-college jaunt to Alaska on somebody's fishing boat. The deadwater creek in West Texas where my long-term boyfriend and I dropped our plans to get married like so many stones. My first trip to Russia: the traditional bathhouse outside our host's dacha where we sweated in herb-scented steam, our glistening skins whipped with birch twigs before we dove into an icy, round lake under pale midnight sun.

Then there was the July afternoon during which, nine months pregnant, I lolled in a neighbor's pool, awed by my body's new buoyancy. I was able to float in any position, adrift in a warm, liquid world like the baby inside me. Twelve hours later, my waters broke, drenching my sheets with the fluids of birth.

Water heals. It soothes and transforms us. One of my friends calls the pool in her yard her significant other. I know what she means. In the water I move like a trout: a secret, more sexual self of effortless grace and impossible confidence. I am porpoise-bold, lithe as an otter, my skin phosphorescent. I would like other people to know her, this deep-water self, but mermaid-like, she refuses to leave her own element.

Still, she is there every time I dive through the surface, closing my eyes for that first stunning immersion, that shedding of skins. Even when I am plodding repetitive laps in the pool of a gym, there is some breathless nymph in my veins. I can never keep count of my laps. I go dreamy in water; my mind floats away from the rhythm of numbers and into a flow of soft image, of instinct and memory.

Some summers ago, I brought my then two-year-old daughter to play at the beach. Veteran of a Y.M.C.A. Water Babies course, she nevertheless showed no interest in testing the water. For hours she puttered and sculpted wet sand, shaping castles and pools with a trowel. And then, in one heart-stopping instant, she lifted her arms in a sky-wide embrace and went barreling into the surf, the living, exuberant image of that long-lost snapshot. My camera was nowhere in sight, but no matter: I couldn't have moved. Tears stung at my eyes, tiny oceans. "Some pictures, you take with your memory," my grandmother told me, and she was right. This one, I know, will be with me forever.

The Perfect House

Laura Shaine Cunningham

The search for the perfect house went on for ten years. Every weekend, I scoured the Sunday *New York Times* real estate section. Certain phrases lured me—"fenced for horses", "former grist mill". The Times functioned as mulch for my imagination (later the newspaper would serve as the real thing, buried between layers of soil). Mentally, I traveled as far north as Maine and as deep south as Maryland.

When I ventured forth to investigate the properties, the shocks multiplied faster than the listings. No place lived up to its description. The perfect dairy barn on the Delaware wasn't on it—it had been under it.

"Well," said the realtor, as she tried to explain the watermarks that ran round the room, like a border motif, "this is the flood plain." The water had not risen that high in more than a decade, the owner insisted. But the scent of mildew filled the house, the floor felt soggy underfoot. A sump pump sat in the cellar, wheezing and spewing the moisture that seeped through the house. The structure, for all its Colonial charm, seemed to be weeping: Fluid streaked down the cheeks of the walls. "We call this 'internal rain,'" the realtor said.

Every perfect house had an unforeseen flaw. My husband and I saw a pre Civil War homestead in Putnam County that boasted a personal footbridge over its private moat. We were smitten, but I became suspicious when the broker drove us to and from the property by a circuitous route. On my own, I walked to the back acres and spotted what she had tried to hide: a small nuclear facility, derby shaped, with red and white carnival-striped stacks. Ground zero. Who cared now, for the original cooking hearth, the random floors, the sewing nook? Radioactivity seemed to float, iridescent among the dust motes, through the spring sunshine.

The search became a *raison d'être*. I toured three states, seven counties. I was looking for something that was, the brokers insisted, impossible to buy. An old house set off the road, with several acres and complete privacy.

"Complete privacy no longer exists," I was told, "not in your price range." Only Wall Street billionaires, rock stars, movie moguls or prizefighters could buy seclusion. The most that I could hope to attain would be "some privacy," advised the Queen of the Brokers.

"There is no such thing as 'some' privacy," I argued. "A place is private or it is not." She fought back, citing "privacy on the side" or "privacy to the back." I vetoed these conditions, foreseeing a future in which I would have to slink from my home in only a single direction. My privacy criterion was strict—I must know that I could walk outside my front door in a nightgown or less without being in plain view of my neighbors. It's not that I expected to be walking out naked very often—I just needed to know that it was possible.

Therefore, before I could find a house, I had to find a compatible realtor. The first realtors I knew seemed formed in a mold—they wore lacquered hairdos, sunglasses and carried designer purses that snapped shut. It was a succession of blind dates with unlikely women. I recall a single male realtor and the odd tension that accompanied us on our tours of bedrooms and toilets. In the hush of empty homes, I could imagine how sometimes realtors might mate with the would-be buyers.

The male realtor was a former male model and he had an odd habit of posing in each room he showed me—I suppose to enhance the image of the future life I might lead with my husband. "Here I am," he seemed to say, "coming in from work, heading for the wet bar. Here I am, helping you in the kitchen." He was married, but unhappily, he told me, to a woman who had been hit by a telephone truck and lost the use of part of her foot, the heel.

The realtor I spent the most time with was a diligent woman nicknamed Pippy, who dominated the listings in a county an hour from New York. She looked like a human magnification of the terrier she sometimes carried: Pippy wore a matching topknot in her hair, and her hairline would move forward in excitement whenever we sniffed out a new listing. She usually wore fur and wafted Joy perfume. "You're going to have to add a couple of zeros" is all she would say. My dream of finding that unspoiled house for under $200,000 was unrealistic. "I got that for an unrenovated dog kennel," Pippy reported toward the end of our relationship.

"Was it private?" I heard myself ask.

Next, I met a former actress (the woods are filled with them), Nancy, a peppy redhead who would stop at road kills and skin raccoons for their fur. I was farther north, and this seemed a part of the riskier frontier setting.

What I liked about going around with Nancy was that she was one of the few realtors who didn't fool around with me on the privacy issue. She did not show me the places with "some" privacy. In fact, a few of the places that she took me to were too private.

The standout in this department was "the estate of Gunther Mueller," a deceased former Nazi who had built a house that could be cleaned by a central hose. The floors slanted toward a main drain, as some shower rooms and slaughter houses do. The estate of Gunther Mueller was private; he had built it bunker-like into the side of the mountain.

The acreage was well defended by chain-link fencing. The rotweilers who had once occupied the barbed wire dog-runs were now gone, as was Gunther, but an aura of militaristic madness remained.

"You could plant morning glories over the chain-link," was Nancy's suggestion. Her next selection was a Cotswold cottage with a private waterfall. The cottage, made of stone, was set far, far back on a dirt road. A family sat in catatonic quiet at their kitchen table with a giant Akita named Bo. I could see an alarm system had just been installed: floodlights aimed at the house. What had happened here? "It won't affect you," was all Nancy would say.

As we went into reverse, Nancy, in an unanticipated turn, began to quote from the Book of Revelation. I had not guessed, until that moment, that she was a Born Again Broker. I gathered from her singsong incantations that even as she tried to sell plots of earth, she felt we were doomed.

So one can see that I did not jump for my car keys, when almost a year later, another realtor called to tell us about the perfect house. We had, in fact, almost given up looking when a broker called in real estate heat. "You must come up here right away," she said. "This one's going to go."

My husband and I resisted. It was raining, we had colds. We were preparing our income tax returns. The last house I'd seen had made the "estate of Gunther Mueller", the dead Nazi, look charming. I did not jump for the car keys. But her voice burbled on in my ear, "Don't you remember? Two years ago? That driveway that we passed and I said –'Doesn't it look like England down there? That's an English estate'. And you said, 'Thomas Hardy! *Far From the Madding Crowd*?'"

I felt a wave of telepathy through the phone, as if the line could also conduct the broker's sincerity. "I kid you not," she said. "This is the one you have spent ten years looking for...This is..." she paused, "a house that Eleanor Roosevelt would have bought."

I grabbed the car keys and my umbrella. My husband wrapped himself in a blanket and said, "You're driving."

A hundred miles later, in a downpour, we turned into the driveway and saw the realtor had spoken the truth. I felt my heart beat against my raincoat, as we entered the maple-lined drive.

Here, even the rain seemed cosmetic, a silver scrim through which we could see a series of buildings that comprised a classic English-style country estate. A white fog floated before the first house, The Manor, and drifted past The Casino, a Victorian "play" house and the carriage barns. Far down the driveway, peeking over a knoll, was " the Inn" , the house we had come to see.

Deer appeared in the fog and stepped daintily out of our way. The animals, luminous eyed, regarded us. "Who are you?" they seemed to ask. "What are you doing here?"

"The Inn" was a squared-off Colonial, painted pale yellow. The house seemed to wink welcome to me, from behind its many shuttered windows. The realtor had not lied—this was a house that Eleanor Roosevelt would have liked. It was beautiful, with its gray and white porches but not 'too fancy." The Inn was set on thirteen acres, most of the property given over to a sloping pasture to the west. The pasture was in use—a herd of Holsteins could be seen, heads lowered to munch the first shoots of spring onion. Beyond my imaginings and almost past comprehension were the outbuildings—a matching barn and the stone foundation of another structure, into which had been set a tennis court. I would have settled for much less, I thought, as I stepped from the car, already saying "yes," as the broker had predicted.

We told the brokers that we would be happy to give the sellers, an English Lord and Lady who still lived in the Manor, their asking price. But was it truly possible to buy this place? Orphans from the Bronx didn't end up in houses like this. Or did they?

I saw the house in a trance of desire. I walked from room to room—there were at least eighteen, more if one counted the third floor "servant's quarters" with its nooks tucked under the eaves. Toward the back of the second floor, I stepped across what appeared as a seam in the wide board floors, the dividing line between the original house and an 1899 addition. The addition was actually a second house, called The Innlet. The two houses were joined, like Siamese twins, at the head. I walked through a Victorian linen closet to reach the back three guest bedrooms. Everything—from the long silver keys, to the stacks of starched monogrammed linens—struck me as perfect. Could we really buy it?

"The Lord is pretty choosy," the realtor told us. 'You will have an interview."

The next weekend we appeared at The Manor. The Lord was the grandson of the founder of the estate, which was called Willowby Park. His grandfather had been an American businessman named Edmund Talbot. Legend had it that Edmund Talbot had stopped at The Inn and been so entranced by his surroundings, that he decided to purchase the Inn and all the adjoining property. In 1892, he built his own house, The Manor, with its outbuildings, The Casino and the carriage barn. According to local history, Talbot then hired the firm of Fredric Law Olmsted to unite all the preexisting farms into the pastoral, English-style park. Of course, I recognized the name Olmsted as the designer of Central Park.

Lord Hodgeson had been selling off chunks of the property in the past few years— he'd already parted with the dairy farm that had made up the Eastern side of the property and a historic stone house that was set to the north end. But the realtor warned me that The Inn was dear to the family, and his Lordship would be particular as to whom they sold the place, if they sold it at all. They had already withdrawn from one would be buyer. The house was not quite officially on the market. My husband and I dressed for the interview. I wore a 1940's plaid coat, with a Harrod's label, that I'd found in a vintage clothing store on Columbus Avenue. I was a playwright and I guessed that the right costume could not hurt.

"What excellent tweed," were the Lord's first words to me as we stepped inside the Manor. It was early spring, but inside, the house retained the chill of the past winter. The thermostat was kept low, just above the temperature at which veneer can crack.

The Lord and Lady led us past a Della Robbia in the main marble hall to a sitting room, where we took our places on an antique sofa. A small fire crackled in the grate. My husband caught my eye and we both almost laughed in relief. We were surrounded by objects and furnishings that the Lord and his antecedents had assembled. Much of the carpet and all the golden silk upholstery was frayed, but this wear added a gloss of beauty and authenticity. A set designer could not have conjured up a more perfect English country house.

I felt as if I might have stepped into a hybrid British play—a cross between *Hay Fever* and *The Bald Soprano*, half drawing room comedy, half inspired farce. Lord and Lady were also perfectly cast as themselves—one could not find a better type than Lord Edmund Hodgeson—fine aquiline features, parchment white skin, a tall bony build. Lady Marguerite was a bit more off-beat— Swedish by birth, she had acquired her husband's British accent and manner, but her eyes, slightly slanted above high cheekbones flashed with the merry beauty she must have been when she attracted the Lord's attention. The Hodgesons were not old, in fact, they were slim and attractive, yet they seemed to belong to another time period. Their faces looked blanched, as if they had just come into the glare of the current year and been a bit taken aback. They seemed as if they, like out-of-season flowers, had been nipped by a killing frost.

Lord and Lady were drinking Cutty Sark. "Our anti freeze," Lady Marguerite said, cupping her hands around the tumbler. The Lord touched on the religious connection between The Inn and a famous celibate monk, Swami Vivekananda, who visited in 1899. "He blessed two women in the house. The Inn still has a special aura. Well, you'll see."

"We lived there for a time ourselves," Lady Marguerite added. "When the children were small. It was bliss." They both sighed, recalling how much cheaper the Inn had been to heat.

"The Inn is snug," they said together.

The Lord escorted us on a tour of the grounds. He donned kid gloves and carried a small crop. As he led us down a hidden path behind The Manor, he flicked away branches of poison ivy that might otherwise have grazed him. "You brute," he said, to the offending vine.

Lord Hodgeson led us down a winding path, over a small plank footbridge to a secluded swimming pond. The pond was concealed by weeping willows and followed a cleft in the landscape. The pond emptied into a stream that, in turn, fed into a meadow where more cows could be seen, posed as if for a painting. I "oohed and aahed," while my husband shushed me, fearful I would jinx the sale or raise the price. But the Lord and Lady accepted our offer of their asking price—a modest one, even in 1981. In return, we vowed to honor the Lord's restrictive covenants, which would be revealed later, in full detail, in our deed. He gave us the gist: "No subdivision, noxious smells, sounds or lights that could glare into the windows of The Manor. No motorcycles, no snowmobiles, no salting the road for winter ice," and so on.

I noticed that the word "noxious" was often repeated along with "objectionable." Sometimes, Lord Hodgeson used both words in the same sentence. When he showed us "our" rosa rugosa bushes, he said, "In summer, you'll be subjected to the Japanese beetles mating two and three at a time on your rosebuds—it's so objectionable—and then, if you must kill them in a Bag-A-Bug, you must dispose of their noxious remains."

In the heat of purchase, we also promised to pay our share of the care for dozens of old sugar maples that lined The Avenue, as His Lordship called the main driveway. We almost skipped up the winding path to the Manor. I could smell the soil as the sun warmed it. Robins tugged at worms. Bona fide Eastern bluebirds flew past in azure pairs and sat on perches to twitter at us.

We and the house were sold. The Lord would hold the mortgage at twelve and a half percent. I envisioned him actually holding it, as a yellowed parchment scroll, in his fine-boned white hands.

Three months later, my husband and I drove up at sunset to take possession. It was July 2 and the grounds were now almost violently verdant, the sugar maples heavy-headed. Across the pasture, the cows walked single-file, the lead cow's bell clanging melodically.

The air was still with the moist heat of near evening and a shocking pink streaked across the Western sky. For a moment, everything we saw was rose-tinted, even the cows. The roses themselves were in bloom, a thousand flowers on the old rugosa hedge that grew in front of the house.

As the light faded, I stood looking at the hedge roses and the lawn beside them seemed to come alive. The Japanese beetles, as predicted by His Lordship, emerged from their winter's hibernation and whirred through the air before alighting on the rose petals and eating them.

Sandcastles

Werner Hengst

Almost every day, my mother and I walked down the beach road, she carrying a bag full of snacks and I running ahead impatiently. In the summer of 1941 I was five years old and the beach was my favorite place in the whole world. The Baltic Sea was only a ten-minute walk from our house in Peenemünde, Germany. On weekends, my father joined us if he could get away from his work.

My father had rented a *strandkorb* or beach basket for the season. But it looked like a huge easy chair. Made from heavy-duty wicker, its back curved up and over to make a roof. The sides came up to meet the roof and form an enclosure open only to the front. The seat, upholstered and covered with green and white striped canvas, was just wide enough for Mutti, Vati and me. Under the flip-up bench, a large storage space was full of sand toys, rolled-up straw mats, sun-shade umbrellas and, of course, a shovel.

All up and down the shore, *strandkorbs* sat about a hundred feet apart on the soft white sand above the high-tide line. In spite of their size, their wicker construction made them light enough to be turned toward or away from the sun, depending on whether shine or shade was desired. Each one had a white number painted on its side, and a padlock to protect the contents of the under-seat storage.

The *strandkorb* marked *our* piece of the beach. My father had shoveled a mound of sand all around it, so tall that I could see over it only by jumping. The mound was called a *strandburg* or beach castle and every *strandkorb* was surrounded by one. Each family took pride in the size and quality of their burg. My mother and I had decorated ours with seashells and pieces of driftwood, especially around the gap on the landward side that served as an entrance. The space was as private as if it had been a room in our house. I had been told never to go into another family's *strandburg*, unless invited.

But there was lots of visiting among the ladies. While my mother chatted with her friends or read her book, I played in the sand, sometimes by myself, sometimes with other kids. We dug holes as deep as our arms could reach or until the bottom filled up with water. Then we brought little handfuls of soft drizzly sand to the surface and made them into elaborate sandcastles. If you let the watery mixture trickle through your fingers, little round lumps of sand would stick together and pile up into fantastic towers that looked like the dripping wax of a candle. They reminded me of pictures I had seen of cave stalagmites. During the night, the tide would make the beach smooth again. At first, I was sad that the sea had destroyed all my work. But then I realized that it had merely given me a clean slate to create new castles and towers. I loved those infinitely long summer days when the world stood still and silent, except for Mutti's voice, asking now and then if I wanted a sandwich or a glass of juice.

Once or twice a month, a loud roar like rolling thunder would come from a spot way down the beach. Thick clouds of dark smoke would boil up from the source of the roar. Sometimes, a thin white streak, jagged like a bolt of lightning, would rise from the smoke and disappear out to sea. "The beach is smoking again," was all Mutti would say in reply to my eager questions. The way she immediately went back to reading her book gave me a clue that further inquiries were not welcome. When I asked my dad about it later, I got the same answer. So, to my growing store of information about the world, I added this: beaches sometimes erupt in loud noises, dark smoke and white streaks of lightning, and grown-ups don't like to talk about it. I did wonder, though, why the mysterious roaring and smoking always seemed to come from more or less the same place and what would happen if the beach suddenly decided to "smoke" closer to us. Maybe, I thought, that was why my mother had refused to tell me more. She didn't want to frighten me with a danger she could do nothing about.

On every visit, Mutti and I roamed up and down the hard-packed sand, holding hands, our bare feet splashing in the surf. I stretched my strides as long as I could, and she shortened hers so that we could walk in step with each other. I had seen films of soldiers marching in step, as a team, and I liked walking like that with my mother. It gave me a grown-up feeling, as if we were doing something important together. Along the way we always collected more shells and interesting objects to add to our beach castle. When my dad came on the weekend, we would proudly show off our finds.

One Sunday late that summer, a terrible storm blew in from the north. My dad went down to the shore to see about our *strandkorb*, followed after a while by my mother and me. When we got to the beach, the sight made me tighten my grip on Mutti's hand. The Baltic Sea, normally tranquil and peaceful, had turned into a wild beast. As far as my eyes could see, breakers were rolling in, pushing huge masses of yellowish foam before them. Every now and then, the wind tore loose a great lump of the foam and sent it rolling up the beach, all the way to the top of the dunes where it would hang up in the tall beach grass. I wanted to run over and touch it, but my mother wouldn't let me go.

Our *strandkorb,* and all the others, had been engulfed by the flood. It was leaning at a crazy angle, half submerged in the sand as the waves smacked into it. The sand berm surrounding it, including all our fancy decorations, had been washed away. It was frightening to see how my gentle, friendly playground had suddenly become so violent and dangerous. My dad said that he and some other men had tried to drag one of the *strandkorbs* up the beach, but it was no use. It was firmly stuck in the sand and would require a machine to lift it out. My mother thought the ocean was simply taking back its property. The wind and spray from the sea made us feel so cold that we were happy to leave our *strandkorb* to its fate and hurry back home. I was glad when we reached our front door and got out of the biting wind. My mother whipped up some of her hot chocolate and I felt warm and cozy again.

Once, the following summer, a friend of my dad's took Mutti and me and several other people on his motorboat for a picnic on a small nearby island. I liked the speed of the boat and the powerful sound of the engine that made the deck vibrate. Sometimes, a sudden cold spray would blow into the boat and the women squealed. But I enjoyed the taste of the salty water on my face and only laughed. When I got to steer the boat for a while and learned to follow a compass heading, things seemed to be about as good as they could get.

Then they got even better. As we sat under some trees on the island, munching our sandwiches, we heard the sound of a small airplane that soon landed in the pasture right in front of us. When the pilot climbed out and took off his goggles, I couldn't believe my eyes. It was my dad! He walked over to us, kissed Mutti and me and had a bite to eat. Then he took me and a couple of other boys to show us the cockpit with its instruments and controls. We didn't really understand what we saw, but it sure was impressive. I had not known that my dad could fly a plane. For the first time, I think, I was proud that he was my father and that the other boys knew he was my father. I hadn't seen much of him, because he was always busy with his work. But now, suddenly, he was more than the tired, grumpy man who rarely had time for me. As he turned the plane around and took off, we all cheered and waved good-bye, and he waggled his wings a couple of times in reply. When I looked up at my mother, she had a tear in her eye, but she was smiling at the same time.

Later, we went to pick some of the sun-warmed blackberries that grew wild all over the island. In a clearing, we found a large burnt-out barn. Our guide said that it had been struck by lightning. Only the big upright timbers were still standing. The roof and walls had collapsed or been consumed by the fire, and lots of weeds and bushes had sprung up among the debris. The smell of burned wood still hung about the place and a vague feeling of horror came over me. In the middle of the floor sat a piece of farm machinery, sagged into itself from the heat of the blaze. Its rust-covered metal frame reminded me of the skeleton of some huge dead animal. A vine with large trumpet-shaped white flowers had twined itself all around and through the bones.

That winter, everyone in our town was busy making preparations against air raids. Peenemünde was, as I learned later, the site of Germany's World War II rocket research. The mysterious smoke I had seen on the beach came from rocket test firings. My father was an officer in the German Air Force, in charge of optical instruments. Because of the work he and the other scientists were doing, my parents were sure that, sooner or later, we would be hit by an air attack. It was only a matter of time. All around the town, I saw crews of men painting the roofs and walls of the houses an ugly dull black to make them less visible from the sky. All our windows were covered with blackout paper, and in our basement, workmen built a "bomb-proof" shelter that was to be our refuge if the bombs started to fall.

To me, it seemed impossible that our big, solid house, my school and all the other large buildings around town could be destroyed by things dropped from an airplane. I had seen my dad fly a plane, and it just didn't seem big enough. But then I remembered what had happened to our *strandburg* and I wasn't so sure.

When the attack actually came the following August, it was worse than anyone had imagined. The air raid sirens wailed and my mother tore me out of my bed and hastily put some clothes on me. There wasn't time to let me do it in my own slow seven-year-old way. Vati snatched up the briefcase with our "important papers" that was permanently parked by our front door, and we ran down the stairs into the basement. In a split-second decision that, it turned out, saved our lives, my father by-passed the bomb shelter and ran out the back door into the open. There, we scrambled down into a covered trench that had been dug into the sandy soil.

Even though the raid lasted only forty minutes, it seemed to go on forever. We huddled together, my head in my mother's lap, my father's arms around both of us. Wave after wave of bombers passed overhead. Each time, we would hear the steady drone of many engines, getting closer and closer. Then, there was the whistle of the falling bombs, a shrill chorus with a descending pitch, and then the impacts that shook the ground. Strange acrid odors filled the air, and the noise was about a million times louder than any thunder I had ever heard. My mother had draped her coat over me, but my eyes hurt from the brilliant flashes of the explosions. Some were so close that the shock waves felt as if someone had punched me in the chest. It took a minute or so before I could breathe normally again. As soon as the engine noise of one wave faded away, the rising roar of another would start up, over and over and over. I don't know how many there were, but I read later that the Peenemünde raid was carried out by 800 bombers and was the biggest of the entire war.

There came a time when we heard no more engines and no more explosions. But we sat still for a long time, dazed and worried that this was only a pause. Finally, we carefully crawled out of the trench. All around us, fires were burning and huge swirling clouds of sparks and embers were rising into the smoky sky. One large block of apartments was blazing in a solid wall of flames. But men were still running in and out of the ground floor, trying to save a few possessions. When the roof collapsed with a huge eruption of sparks, some of the women screamed, afraid that their husbands were inside.

We started to look for our house, but couldn't find it. Vati told me later that it had been hit by a 2000-pound bomb, which simply had blown it away with everything we owned, including the bomb shelter, my new bicycle and all my toys. All that was left was a six-foot high pile of rubble, topped by a thin sliver of wall leaning at a weird angle. The wall was covered with white tiles and our bathroom sink was dangling from it by a pipe. Where our front door had been, only three stone steps remained, leading into empty space.

The three of us stood among the blowing smoke and dust for a long minute, hugging each other. My father still gripped the important briefcase, which, except for the clothes we had on, was our only possession. The bombs had taken away our house and most of our town just as easily as a wave on the beach could wash away one of my sandcastles.

Though I didn't fully understand it at the time, it was a lesson about the impermanence of material things that I would never forget.

Short Story

Bones Like Ice

James P. Othmer

"My brother talked me into joining. Not so much talked me into it, but forced me to go along 'cause he wasn't more than a boy and he needed watching. Either way your mother was not happy about me going. We'd just started the farm and just had another child. I told her I'd rather join and be with my brother than be conscripted later with strangers. Many men did not serve at all, including some of the very same civic leaders who give patriotic speeches and pass judgment on me today, because they found doctors who would confirm an old weakness, or consumption, or a foul knee. Later they'd be able to buy their way out for $300. But I couldn't afford that, or a doctor. Besides I had my brother to protect and in truth I felt an excitement about what adventure might lie ahead that to this day I'm ashamed of. In 1862 everyone had dreams of glory, but that all changed by '63. After the first brush with real war all but the craziest dreamed of nothing but home and peace. By the time we reached Cedar Creek in the fall of '64, we had seen action near Gettysburg and Petersburg and Harper's Ferry. We had been away from our kin for two years. We had seen more versions of death than a sane mind can handle. I saw boys I grew up with die in a flash and die for what seemed an eternity, lying in fields too close to the Rebel pickets to be saved. And soon I would see much worse.

"Here is another view of it. From the home you lived in then: Every week I received a letter from your mother. For two years she raised four children and tried to run the farm that took up all the money we had and were to have for years to come. At first I lived for her letters. They were filled with love and encouragement. I found gold in the smallest of details and begged her to share them. Were they thrashing the oats? Had the leaves turned on the big maple? Anything about the children, about you. But with time the letters changed. The winters were harsh. The children were a burden for a woman alone. Food was scarce and the relief money the town provided the families of soldiers was not enough. I sent home all I could, but she was losing her grip on the farm. In late-September she wrote that baby Cynthia was not well and asked for me to get leave to come home.

"We had just skirmished with Early at Opequon Creek and then again at Berryville. The battles are not famous, but the fighting was as fierce as the ones of legend. Just smaller numbers of men killing high percentages of each other. After we routed the Rebs at Winchester it looked like we had them whipped for the year and probably for good in the Shenandoah. I requested furlough the next day and was denied. No one was to be given leave until we drove the Rebs out of the Valley. I thought of the farm all the time. Soon after we fought and won at Fisher's Hill. When not fighting or preparing to fight we were ordered by Sheridan to turn the Valley into a barren waste. We killed the land, burning crops and mills. Barns. Grain. Taking the last livestock from families just like ours. We did not leave them with an ounce of bread, meat or firewood. As barns burned and smoke fouled the sky, I felt more like a criminal than a soldier. I wrote home that we'd soon prevail in the Valley and I'd be home as soon as possible. At night by the fire I shook so much I needed two hands to hold my coffee tin.

"On the morning of October 18, my brother, Richard, was picked to go on a foraging party to the south of Cedar Creek. I thought of volunteering to replace him but my mind was on home and the farm. At noon a mail wagon arrived. The letter from your mother said that Cynthia's fever had worsened and she feared for her life. I sat in my tent and cried. All along I had thought I would rather my children mourn my death than my disgrace, but I knew I had to go home. I packed my haversack and sat waiting for Richard to return. Just before dusk he did. Behind the small group of infantrymen was a wagon pulled by a team of mules. Richard's body lay in the wagon beside a carpenter from Somers and a saloonkeeper from Poughkeepsie.

"I guess you could say that I had something of a breakdown. I went to my commanding officer, Major Compton, from the bank in town, and begged him to let me go home. He had let others go for lesser reasons, but he refused me and told me I would be shot if I tried. There was bad blood between us from before the war, almost from the time you were born. It didn't matter anymore, though. I left camp before dawn.

"That morning, with the fog spilling across the creek and the valley floor, filling the hollows, my first steps were not away from but toward something. Toward my sick child, my family and my farm. But it is never that simple. Because anyone who runs toward something is also running away from something. It all depends on how you see it.

"The Rebels surprised us, rushing across the creek at dawn and routing our left flank. Thousands were startled and driven from their tents that morning, but I was tagged a coward because the Major had noticed I was missing minutes before the first bullet flew. I wasn't yet to the Valley Pike when I heard the first volleys. I stopped to listen, thinking it was no more than a skirmish, but soon our men came racing toward me, half-dressed and many without weapons. I turned and ran with them. At some point we stopped and formed a line. The story goes that Sheridan raced up the pike to rally us and maybe he did. But I never saw him and even if I had I would not have rallied and returned fire because of the hat waving of an officer. I fought because we were going to die if we did not.

"My mind blurs here, but I know we started something of a counter charge. I was struck first in the thigh, just above the knee, and had begun to crawl toward the shelter of a tree when a minié ball passed through the inside bend of my elbow, taking the knot of the joint with it on the way out. There was smoke and screams and the sound of metal ripping the air. The moans of the living and the silence of dead. I sat crying, holding what was left of my arm and hoping that death would come swiftly as the last major battle in the Shenandoah unfolded before me. The gunfire and artillery continued, relentless, but I was beyond fear. I thought of my brother, my daughter. All of us at dinner on the farm. Soon the last of the men who had charged with me retreated right back past me again, and for a while the shooting ceased, and there was a silence like a dream as I sat alone in the fog and smoke of the field. I was surrounded by dead and dying, but after a while you get accustomed to the screams of the dying, and it becomes part of the silence.

"Soon the Rebels came out of the woods, hollering as they swarmed past. Some knelt beside me to take aim, and one young man fell dead with a bullet in the chest that I heard hit like a fist. I held my arm and cried and listened to the bullets of my own army whistle past. With the next wave of Rebels came the scavengers. These men had no boots on their feet and many wore the coats of Union soldiers. They were bone-thin and hollow-eyed. One stopped and took my boots, commenting when he saw my knee that I wouldn't need them anymore, anyway. They took my ammunition, my belt, my last plugs of tobacco. A boy not much older than you took the blanket from my haversack and said, "Sorry, Yank." I couldn't speak, could only look at him. After a moment, he considered me with different eyes, then ripped a rag from his trousers and tied it around my arm just below the shoulder. Probably saved my life but not my arm. Soon after the Union counter charge would come, and everyone who had run one way would run the other again. It struck me that this is what the war had become. Running back and forth, killing each other over vacant strips of land. I came to in a field hospital as they were taking off the rest of the arm. There's no need to describe that, unless you'd like. One thing I'll tell you is that I watched it all. For some reason I thought if you looked straight on at that kind of bad there would be nothing to be afraid of again. While if you closed your eyes to it, you'd see it forever. But I still see it. Sometimes I feel it more than when it was there. And I still fear many things.

"Two days later in a hospital in Maryland I was handed a letter from your mother telling me that our Cynthia had died. By the time I got home your mother had had a breakdown of her own that has come and gone ever since. You must never blame her for what she's become. While I was gone she stayed and tried to save the family. We once had dreams like every boy and girl you'll ever know. Before we became an embarrassment we had been a couple that made people feel good just watching us walk past.

"When I finally came home the war was over and there was a parade for our regiment and a great many speeches. It was called a great war and a monument was unveiled in town with Lincoln's words on it near the very spot where our leaders had denounced Lincoln and the war in '60 and again in '64 when he did not even carry the vote in our county. When I finally had to go to the bank to try to save the farm they refused to help me. Compton had told everyone his story, which no doubt varies from mine. With so many people prospering elsewhere you wonder why I didn't pack us up and leave. I considered it, but there was no way. Physically. Financially. Not to mention the state your mother and I were in.

I know you don't think much of me. You see men getting rich all around you and you want in on it. You want me to be like them. But I can't. I've had to settle for more modest ambitions. You want me to make you proud, but that's really up to you, Henry. Make your own story as good as you can, son, because my part of it's told and done."

* * *

A rogue squall lashes snow against the side of the shanty. Henry rises stiff-legged and shivering. The shanty is empty, the fire out. He touches his boot-tops, then wraps his arms around himself. His hands tremble as he struggles to put on his gloves. He thinks of his father's tale, the longest he's ever heard the old man speak, and tries to separate what was truth and dream, because even now, opening the door to the blue wall of the coming dawn, he feels less than awake. The squall has passed and he looks up to see that Venus is gone, dropped into the sky of another place. Saturn is the morning star, but he doesn't notice it in the bluing heavens. Snow crunches under his boots like small bones breaking. He knows now that he was wrong about his father. For years he had hoped he was wrong, that there was a reason that he wasn't as ambitious, as successful as just about everyone else, but now that he knows he was wrong it feels worse than if he had been right. He thinks of his father crying in that unfamiliar field, clutching his shredded arm, knowing that his brother lay dead and untended in an abandoned cart close by and his daughter lay alone in her baptismal dress in the smallest of graves far away. When he reaches the lake he sees the abandoned spud pole and the channel glassed over and clear-sealed like the portal to another world, and he knows that his father is down there beneath the newly formed surface, drifting in the slack tide of an endless dream. And it doesn't matter whether he slipped or jumped, dived headfirst or eased into it like it was a soothing bath. He is down there and it is not his fault.

He stands at the edge of the frozen lake, watching the pale luminance to the east. A flickering yellow in the sunless sky. Watching miniscule debris from the first moment of time, remnant silicate dust from the creation of compacting planets, the expanding bow of space, swirling in some other time and for all time. Watching the rays of the still-hidden sun bouncing off these original grains appearing now on his horizon in a broad glowing arc. It is a false dawn, the rare chafe of a moonless night, intricate steps of celestial choreography, but to Henry the bright glow resembles nothing less than the hard-burning lights of a thriving metropolis just over the next hill. He imagines the pulse and swagger of such a world, watches its kinetic shimmer until it vanishes in the day's true light.

At the edge of the channel he picks the bar up off the plank, wraps his gloved hands around its shaft and, with the first tears that he cannot will away, he begins to chop at the thin pane of ice. Chops with the beveled edge of the cold iron, ice shattering like glass. Chops until there's room enough to drag the float through the passage he'd been charged with keeping open.

The 3-Mile Run

Anthony Robinson

As I crossed our yard that drizzly afternoon, home from school, smoke was rising from the ground where my father, over the weekend, had burned out a tree stump. For the last couple of years he'd worked on making a lawn, and that required clearing the ground. It was slow work and I didn't see much progress except for a patch of grass the size of a ping-pong table. Our house sat among a lot of oaks and hemlocks and today, especially, looked sad and lonely. I had a feeling that something had happened. Then it hit me. We'd lost another boy in West Harleyville.

I pushed open the front door, walked through the living room and into the kitchen. My mother was at the sink peeling potatoes. "Hello, Rupert," she said, not turning around.

I put my books on top of the big chest where we kept pots and pans. "Hi, Mom."

"How was school?" She still hadn't turned around, and her voice seemed tight, caught in her throat.

"It was OK," I said.

I opened the refrigerator for a bottle of milk, and when I set it on the table she was facing me, drying her hands on her apron. She had dark hair, pinned back as always. She was frowning, and her eyes were dark and heavy. I grabbed a glass from the cabinet, poured the milk—

"Rupert," she said, "I have something to tell you. Sit down."

I was right after all. Two months ago my mother had said the same thing, then had told me that Archie Beesmer's B-17 had gone down on a bombing run over Germany. He had given me his Red-Eyed Wobbler for the duration and when the war ended he was going to take me deer hunting. About a week later I saw a gold star after his name on the Roll of Honor in West Harleyville.

"This is very hard for me to say," my mother said, sitting down with me.

"Mom, just tell me, all right?"

She pressed her lips together. "Seth Nichols is dead."

I didn't say anything, just stared at her.

She reached across the table and covered my hand. "At first I wasn't going to say anything, but I spoke to your father and he said you had to know—we had to tell you."

"Mom, what are you saying? Seth's only—he's only fifteen. You can't join up at fifteen!"

"He committed suicide," she said.

"*Committed suicide?*"

"He hanged himself in their house in Chicago."

I gave my head a shake, wanting to cry. "Mom, that's awful. *Why?*"

"They say he was very depressed, possibly because of the war. No one really knows." She was still holding my hand. "I'm sorry, Rupert."

We sat for a couple of minutes without talking. Then I said I was going out.

"Maybe you should stay in," my mother said.

"I'm OK, Mom."

"Where are you going?"

"No place. Just around."

Outside, I moved aimlessly about the yard; with the smoke and the drizzle and the stumps, it had the look of a battlefield. I began walking up Rawson Road. On rainy or very cold days, back then, my mother would drive me to school in West Harleyville, and we would always stop by for Seth who lived just up the road; but most of the time Seth and I walked.

It wasn't long before I came to the trail, the shortcut through the woods we'd taken so many times. I started along it, my thoughts going back to that spring day two years ago...

****

Mr. Myer had just rung the bell ending recess, and eight or ten of us left the field and began walking toward the school. Bill Vitone had the ball in his hand. Its cover had come off the day before, so he'd taken it home and wrapped it with black tape. He flipped the ball to Jimmy Osterhout who tossed it way up, then caught it behind his back. Showing off, like eighth graders were always doing.

The schoolhouse, a dingy yellow, sat on the corner of Hammond Street and Bonesteel Lane. The flag flew out front on a high pole, and parked under a maple was Mr. Myer's brown Plymouth. We took the steps up, dropped our mitts in the hall and went in. Seth was already at his desk. Sometimes he came out at recess, but he didn't like baseball or football, so he never joined in, was never there when we chose up sides. When he'd first come to the West Harleyville school, last September, he'd said he was a runner; he ran "the distances." The kids had laughed. Jimmy Osterhout, who had a nonstop mouth, said the only "distance" Seth ever ran was the distance to the outhouse.

I sat down in the row for sixth graders and Jimmy and Bill went over to their desks, behind Seth's. Mr. Myer announced Eighth Grade Science.

I should've been studying my New York State geography—we

were doing the Erie Canal—but I got wrapped up in the eighth-grade class instead. The topic was gravity. Mr. Myer was talking about Galileo's experiment from the top of the Leaning Tower of Pisa. What did the experiment prove? No one spoke. Then Seth raised his hand. It proved that gravitational pull was the same no matter what an object weighed, he said. Then Seth talked about gravitational pull elsewhere. On some "celestial bodies" it was so strong a penny would weigh a ton. On other bodies so weak you'd be able to lift a car. Personally, I didn't believe it, but Mr. Myer praised Seth for a full and excellent answer.

He turned his back to write on the blackboard and Jimmy Osterhout said something to Bill Vitone, then made a spitball and bounced it off Seth's head. A couple of the kids snickered. Mr. Myer spun around. He had hollow cheeks and a sharp jaw, and he always wore the same dark-blue suit, shiny as coal. Everyone said he had eyes in the back of his head. He told Jimmy to go to his office. Ten minutes later Mr. Myer walked down the aisle, went in and bounced Jimmy off the walls for a couple of minutes. When Jimmy came back to his desk, his shirt tails were out and his hair was all mussed, but he had a smirk on his face and he walked with a swagger. Mr. Myer announced Seventh Grade English. It seemed like a good time to start reading up on the Erie Canal.

Five or six kids were standing on the corner when school got out at three o'clock. Jimmy was for playing a couple of innings, but Bill said the bass in Dewitt Pond were beginning to hit. Fred Longo had taken down the flag, delivered it inside, and soon came out. He had big ears and stringy brown hair and was the only kid in the school I didn't like; he was for fishing. So Jimmy said, OK, fishing. Finally Seth came down the steps carrying his books. He was old-looking for thirteen, with reddish-brown hair and a large head. He trudged over to where I was standing and we started walking away.

"Wait a minute," Jimmy Osterhout said.

"What is it?" I said, stopping.

"Not you, Rupert! *Him.*" Jimmy's small blue eyes leveled on Seth. "I'm calling your bluff."

"What on?" said Seth.

"That you're a distance runner."

"Call it, I don't care," Seth said.

"OK, let's do it then. We'll go around Bonesteel, then down Hammond and back to the school. Right now, you and me."

Bonesteel Lane curved back through the town like a huge horseshoe and hit Hammond four-hundred yards from the schoolhouse corner. It was a good mile and a half.

"All right," Seth said.

"Bill, you start us," Jimmy said.

"In two weeks," Seth said.

"What do you mean, *two weeks?*"

"We'll run in two weeks—only we'll go around twice."

Jimmy didn't say anything right away; he was thinking about it, maybe caught off guard. Then he said, "OK."

Seth and I started walking again, first on Hammond, then down a steep street to Turner's Mill. I liked the smell of the sawdust and fresh-cut lumber. Past the sheds was a big open area where the trucks turned around—and beyond that point a big woods began. Last fall—the first week of school—I'd shown Seth the trail. If you took it, the walk to and from the Rawson Colony was fifteen to twenty minutes; by the main roads, over an hour.

The trail ran along a ridge of thick pines, then dipped, circling a swampy area where hundreds of dead trees stood, totally barkless, like skeletons. Maybe fifty crows were perched in the brittle gray branches of one tree, cawing away. Along the side of the trail, in a damp, shaded patch, pink flowers were growing, maybe two dozen in all. Earlier this spring, when we'd first seen them,

I'd told Seth they were called Lady's Slippers. What they were was wild orchids, I said. He wanted to pick one and bring it to his mother, but I told him they were protected by state law, so he left it alone. A limb moved up ahead in an oak. Gray, I thought. Then, sure enough, a big gray squirrel jumped to another tree. Seth didn't see it. He was walking heavily along, eyes lowered. Last fall, walking home one afternoon, he'd told me he didn't like what was happening in Europe. What was happening in Europe? I asked him. He said "dark clouds" were spreading across the Continent. In his opinion, we were headed for another world war. It was funny how someone could see dark clouds over Europe but not a squirrel in a tree.

A big fallen oak lay across the trail. We sat on it, as we often did. Seth's feet touched, but mine had a couple of inches to go. Off to the right, in a grove of pines, stood a single white birch. It always made me think someone was standing there, watching us. He sat bent over a little. By his expression, I thought he was probably seeing those dark clouds. "Rupert," he said, "I don't care whose side you're on. If you're for Jimmy, that's fine."

"I'm not for Jimmy." It scared me a little saying it, but it was true.

We were quiet for a while. In the pines a squirrel was chattering away. I knew it was a red by the sound, sharp and angry. A gray squirrel makes a softer, sadder sound, like someone crying.

"I'd like you to be my trainer," Seth said.

"Your trainer? I don't know anything about running the distances."

"I'll teach you."

I looked at the tops of my shoes, thinking about the West Harleyville kids, what they'd say if they found out. I could imagine, and didn't like what I imagined.

"How about it, Rupert?"

"Well—sure. OK."

We shook on it, then got up and began walking again. The trail came out on Rawson Road, at the southern end of the art colony. We walked a short way and saw the first cabin. All the cabins had names. Up ahead was "Carpenter Shop." It had a steep roof and a sculptor, Carl Roja, lived in it. He carved big pieces of wood, weird shapes that didn't look like anything *I'd* ever seen. We came to the place where the artists would meet for coffee or supper starting in early June right through to November; it had a big screened-in porch and was called "Intelligentsia." A woman with caramel-colored skin ran it; her name was Christine. I liked stopping by when she was cooking up big crocks of goulash or chili. An old abandoned quarry separated "Intelligentsia" from the next house, called "Bluestone"; it had an exterior of flat stones, fitted together like a jigsaw puzzle. Seth lived here with his mother and father. Two empty pails were sitting at the start of a short path leading to the house.

He almost stumbled over them, but that was the idea. Seth set his books on a flat rock. I had nothing special to do, so I told him I'd help. I grabbed one of the pails and we crossed Rawson Road, then followed a path past Lucy LeBlanc's house. She was an artist who painted pictures of naked women. In one painting seven were sitting around a pool laughing and eating grapes and having a wonderful time. We came to a ridge. Here smaller cabins were scattered through the woods. These were taken by the actors and musicians and artists who came to the colony summers only. My parents and Carl Roja and Seth's parents lived here year round. We reached the pump. It was on the edge of a big yellow field, and at the end of the field stood a large building made of rough timbers and pine slabs. It was the Rawson Concert Hall. It blended in so nicely with the woods you might never know it was there. One of the pails wasn't completely empty, and Seth poured what was left down the throat of the pump to prime it. The pump didn't have an ordinary handle but a big iron pipe, six feet long. Alone, I could hardly budge it.

We both grabbed the pipe and pressed down on it, again and again. After two nonstop minutes the water started flowing, and pretty soon the pails were full. The water was icy cold and Seth was sweating, and he told me to keep the handle going while he put his head underneath; it was a struggle for me, but I managed it. Then he pumped and I got doused.

For a while we sat resting up in the sun letting our hair dry. A hawk was making a big slow circle in the blue sky over Ohayo Mountain. Finally, we got up and I went to reach for one of the pails, but Seth took both—"for balance"—and didn't stop once for a rest. We reached his yard. There wasn't a blade of grass anywhere—just pine needles. Seth was staggering. In a corner of the yard sat the Model T he was trying to make go again; an artist had left it behind five or six years ago as dead. Seth liked to say I was helping him, even though all I did was steelwool rusty parts and pass him tools when his head was buried in the engine.

I held the door to the screen porch and he set the pails under the drainboard in the kitchen, puffing away. Half the main room was his father's studio, the part under the skylight. I looked at the mural Mr. Nichols was working on. It was a train yard, all the engines and cabooses, smoke and coal piles and turntables, the workers and engineers. I thought it was a great painting. Every time I looked at it, I saw something new. On a bench across from Mr. Nichols's paints and canvases lay newspapers and magazines, mostly from New York City. A Chicago paper came in each week, Seth told me, and every two weeks a London paper. And once a month a paper called *Le Monde* arrived from Paris. One time Seth read me an article in French. I didn't understood a single word, naturally, but it was fun listening to him. He taught me three words, "bonjour," "merci" and "au revoir."

"I'll see you in ten minutes, Rupert," he said. "Ride your bike so you can pace me."

At home, I had a glass of milk and talked with my mother. My father was in New York. He was a poet, but to make ends meet he wrote articles for magazines, and he was always seeing editors. We had our own well and the only inside bathroom in the colony.

I went back out, getting my bike from the shed. Seth was waiting for me by my parents' mailbox. Opposite the box was a small field surrounded by woods, and in the center of the field stood the Rawson Horse. A sculptor named Richard Flannery had carved it out of a dead walnut tree before I was born. It was rearing up, its head high, ears back, a wild look in its eyes. My father said it was the symbol of the colony.

Seth told me to stay ahead of him by twenty feet; pacing a runner acted as an incentive, kept him going. "OK," he said, "start." He slogged along, head lowered, in an old pair of corduroys and black, ankle-height sneakers. Boom, boom, boom—he had heavy legs and he jarred the road each time a foot came down. After a while he said, "Move it—out—a little—"

I pedaled faster and Seth ran a little faster. Boom, boom, boom. Finally he stopped, so I stopped. His face was red and he was gasping for breath. He kind of leaned on me, and I figured holding up the runner was part of a trainer's job.

"OK," he said, "now back. We'll pretend—my mailbox is—the finish. When we get—to your mailbox—shout 'kick.'"

"'Kick?'"

"It's an extra—burst of speed—at the end. Just shout it."

I turned my bike around and Seth started running again. Soon he was panting fiercely. I heard a car; you could always hear one coming on Rawson Road, as far away as three miles. By the time of day and the tinny sound it made, it had to be Mr. Levitt in his

Nash. It was; he gave us a honk. Seth was hammering the road and, at my mailbox, I yelled, "Kick!"

I didn't notice any burst of speed. So I yelled it again. "Kick!" Nothing.

The road made a small turn, and when we got to his mailbox—maybe two hundred yards from mine—he stopped running. He staggered and heaved, then clasped his hands behind his head and stumbled along.

"Do you want to sit down and rest?" I asked.

"No. You never—do that. You have to—keep moving."

"Oh." I could hear the low thud-thud of Carl Roja's mallet through the woods.

"We have to—work on—my kick, Rupert," Seth said, still walking. "When you run the distances—it's everything."

"That's what we'll do then."

"Tomorrow, same time," Seth said.

A couple of days later, Jimmy Osterhout asked me, as we were coming in from recess, if anything was going on with Seth. "What do you mean?" I said.

"Is he training?

"Not that I know of."

He scowled; when he scowled he looked like a muskrat. "Walking together, he ever mention anything like strategy?"

"Strategy?"

"How he's going to run the race."

"No."

"What *does* he say to you, walking back and forth?"

"Sometimes he'll ask me about this or that."

"Like what 'this or that'?"

We went up the school steps. "Like a squirrel or a tree."

"What's the matter with you, Rupert?"

"Nothing. Why?"

"Forget it," Jimmy said. He gave me a hard, mean look. We tossed our mitts in the corner and went in. Seth was at his desk, reading a book. Mr. Myer announced Eighth Grade Science. I had a test coming up on the main waterways in New York State, but I couldn't concentrate. I was trying to straighten out a couple of things in my mind, like whose side I was *really* on. Seth was my friend, but I'd known the kids in West Harleyville all my life. Later that day, coming home from school, I saw my father working in the yard. I wanted to talk with him because I knew he'd give me advice, but I didn't say anything; I just stood there watching him trying to finish off a charred stump with a mattock. Then I went in. It was something I had to figure out on my own.

Every day Seth ran and I paced him on my bike. After a week, he didn't stagger so bad at the end and his face didn't get so red. And he started to have a kick too, though not much of one. Then, on Thursday, with only two days before the race, we trained extra hard, because Seth said on Friday we wouldn't do anything. A runner never trained the day before a race.

I pedaled and he thundered along. It was a hot day and the tar patches on the road were starting to bubble. Seth stayed to the side to avoid the tar. He was panting and sweat poured down his face; he was running pretty well, I thought. A whole lot better than the day we'd started. My mailbox was just ahead. I was about to shout "Kick!" But a car was coming down Rawson Road, drawing close, and I decided to let it go by first. It went by, and who had his head sticking through the open window, big ears and all, but Fred Longo.

"Your goose is cooked, Rupert!"

My wheels slipped on the loose gravel, and I went sprawling. Seth stopped running and came over. "You all right?" he said, heaving, his shirt soaked.

I sat on the side of the road, a couple of pebbles in my knee, clenching my teeth. I didn't say anything and Seth helped me up. "You'd better go in," he said.

I pushed my bike away, limping. My mother looked at the scrape and cleaned it with peroxide and put a gauze bandage on it. Friday morning I stayed in bed, telling her I felt sick. She took my temperature. Normal. Still she let me stay home. I thought about all the kids going up the school steps, talking, and how I didn't have the nerve to face them. About ten-thirty I got up and had a bowl of corn flakes and told my mother I was going out for a while. A man and woman were walking along Rawson Road with suitcases and artist equipment, looking for Bear Cub; so I offered to show them where it was. The woman was about twenty-five and had red hair; the man was a little older and had no hair at all. When we got to "Bear Cub," they invited me to come visit whenever I wanted. I walked on, stopping by "Intelligentsia" when I saw the door was open. Inside, sweeping and cleaning up, was Christine. We talked for a long while, and I helped her scrub the tables. Carl Roja was busy making his big wooden sculptures, and I went by Lucy LeBlanc's house and she was tending the flowers in her garden and waved and asked me why I was limping. I told her I'd taken a spill on my bike. Finally, I came to the pump on the ridge. I was thirsty, but knew better than to try working the handle by myself. I walked out to the road again, passing Seth's mailbox; then, in front of my own mailbox, I stopped. On the other side of the road was the Rawson Horse.

I kept looking at it, wondering how anyone could make something so lifelike out of a dead tree, so wild and free. Then, all at once, I knew what I had to do.

The next morning, Saturday, I told my mother I was going to the school. Just to see some of the kids. She told me to take it easy, give my knee a chance to heal. I walked through the woods, then up the steep hill at Turner's Mill to Hammond Street. Maybe sixty people were gathered around Jimmy and Seth at the corner of Hammond and Bonesteel, and not just grade-school kids either. High-school kids and parents, too. Bill Vitone was giving instructions to Jimmy and Seth. Painted on Hammond Street was a white line, which Bill said was both the start and the finish. They were to run twice around, as agreed. Jimmy was fidgety, anxious to get going. Seth stood with his head lowered, never seeing me, in his old corduroys and black high-tops. Then Bill said, "Get ready, get set." He hesitated, then shouted, "Go!"

Jimmy shot ahead. Seth started out like he always did, steady, pounding the road. By the time they disappeared around the bend, Jimmy had a big lead. We waited for them to come around the turn on Bonesteel, on the far side of the big field, but it was only Jimmy we saw. He still had that springy step and the crowd started cheering. At last Seth came into view, and I gave out a big yell. Behind me, two women started talking. "His parents are Communists," one said, almost as if she wanted me to hear. "They're all Communists in the Rawson Art Colony," the other woman said. "There should be a law, it's not right they send their kids here." Jimmy turned at Hammond and ran on the straightaway. People were clapping, giving him encouragement. Seth followed him, head down. *Boom, boom, boom.*

Both started the second lap, the "gun lap," Seth called it. Jimmy disappeared on Bonesteel, Seth also. Everyone was staring across the field, waiting—then we saw them again, Jimmy still leading but only by twenty feet. They rounded the last turn where Bonesteel hit Hammond, heaving, panting, their shirts drenched, faces twisted in pain.

They were getting closer, almost on us, everyone screaming for Jimmy, no one louder than the women behind me. I had never yelled so loud, and didn't think I would ever yell so loud again. "Kick, Seth! *Kick!*"

They were both stumbling, ready to fall. But with ten feet to go Seth pulled ahead and crossed the finish line two steps in front. Silence fell on the West Harleyville crowd like cold, heavy snow.

Both runners were so winded they could hardly get their breath. Friends and classmates clustered about Jimmy. I went over to Seth, who had his hands behind his head, and pretty soon we broke away from the crowd and started up Hammond Street, walking along without talking. After a while his breathing, became steady and his hands fell to his sides. We went down the hill by the lumber yard and into the woods, passing the dead trees and the shaded spot where Lady's Slippers grew. We walked on; ahead, I saw the solitary birch among the pines, and at the fallen oak Seth said we should sit down and rest. He had something to tell me, he said.

He told me his father had received an offer to teach at a college in Chicago, and they were leaving the colony. He thanked me for being his trainer. "I heard you yell 'kick,' Rupert," he said. "It made a difference."

****

Now, two years later, the trail seemed different to me as I trudged along. Since Seth had left, I hadn't walked it once. Up ahead lay the fallen oak. When I got to it, I sat down, barely noticing that my feet reached the ground. For a long time I stared down the trail toward West Harleyville. Then I seemed to feel someone's eyes on my back. I spun around, and there, alone in the evergreens, stood the white birch. I went over to it, and rested my head against it. From somewhere in the woods, I heard the sad and lonely cry of a gray squirrel; but then I realized it wasn't a gray squirrel I was hearing.

Butterfly Kisses

Annecy Baez

    We are driving towards New Jersey, my husband and I, to pick up our seventeen-year-old daughter, who is visiting her father for the weekend. As we drive there, I am suddenly reminded of how much I used to love my ex-husband, particularly when I was seventeen and he taught me how to give him butterfly kisses. His eyelashes would come close to mine and blink once or twice and the soft touch of our lashes would be a reminder of his love. Then it would be my turn and I would do the same to him, my lashes flashing across his lashes until we hugged each other, laughing hysterically. Soon these innocent kisses graduated to more elaborate ones: mouth opening slowly, the touching of tongues, and the warmth of our lips. It was so sweet to love him, so safe, I thought it would last a lifetime, but soon, other lips would take my place and other eyes would learn the pleasure of his kisses.
    When we arrive in New Jersey, out of respect, my present husband waits in the car while I go upstairs. Once there, my kisses fly everywhere, on my daughter's cheeks, the new wife's, and their child, while my ex-husband, standing in the living room, watches us. He's a Dominican man, of Italian, Haitian & French descent. He's tall, dark and fashionable, wearing baggy jeans, with an overpriced black T-shirt and expensive Italian shoes with no socks. I go to kiss him hello and he awkwardly hugs me, his arms dangling around me, forgetting how they once held me, lips barely touching

my cheek and his eyes glancing nervously away from me, embarrassed for what regrets I may find in them. A federal agent with strange hours and secrets he could not share, I left when I was six months pregnant because I couldn't tell his truths from his lies. Four years later, I was married. It wasn't easy.

My daughter goes to the bedroom to pack her bags while my ex-husband and I sit in the living room. His wife offers me something to drink. She's a small woman with large breasts and short auburn hair. She's meek, humble and kind to me. She insists on preparing me some lemonade and disappears to the kitchen. My ex-husband is happy to see me and we sit in the living room to talk. His daughter skips around us, humming a song. She's dark with long, black wavy hair and she smells like bubble gum. Knowing that I only have a few minutes, my ex-husband speaks quickly about everything: the weather, the unending war, and his job for homeland security. His wife comes towards me with the lemonade in a tall sweaty glass that she holds with a white napkin and she hands it to me. She sits at a distance hearing him speak. I listen and think about the war, the dead and missing sons and daughters, about the future and when I sincerely say, "Thanks for trying to keep us all safe," he becomes silent, swallows and then coughs, a gesture that reminds me of the times when he wanted to return to me, but I wouldn't take him back. His eyes would swell with tears, and he would cough as he explained himself, and said I was crazy – "How can you throw away ten great years?" – but I wouldn't listen. He covers his mouth with his fist and coughs again, and his daughter, knowing him like I do, goes to him for a hug and he in response hugs her back. When he is composed, he looks at me and then at her and he says to her jokingly to give me a kiss. He laughs, but the child is surprised and I say, "She already did," and he says to the child, "But give her another one," and I say, "Don't force her."

The child is staring at me wondering what she should do, and then, to my surprise, he says to her, "Then give her a butterfly kiss, like the ones I taught you," and I am breathless at the coincidence as my throat turns to a knot and my heart flutters. My daughter comes from the bedroom, and urges her sister to kiss me too, "Yeah, show her that you can give butterfly kisses like daddy taught us," and I stay there as I watch his daughter come towards me, her small face, so similar to his, and her tiny soft lashes come close to mine and they flutter against each other in a tiny butterfly kiss. I feel a lump in my throat and I manage to say, "Thank you." She smiles and runs towards her father, who is pleased. Nervously, I stand up and I say, "Bueno, me tengo que ir," that I must leave, and he says, "Don't go," and his wife stirs and says, "You're always in a rush."

My ex-husband offers me food, rice, beans, honey and some fruits. My daughter mentions how he buys the best fruits, and my ex-husband begs me to take some. "Nah, I have to go right away," I say, but he takes my hand and takes me to the kitchen while the wife watches.

The house is simple, and immaculately clean. Everything is dusted and the computer has a clear plastic cover. In the kitchen, everything is in its place and in harmony. All of this cleanliness is a part of him. His variety of vitamins are on top of the refrigerator and he speaks about nutrition and health, explaining the power of Zinc, DHEA and CQ10. He opens the ultra-clean refrigerator and gets the reddest apple I've ever seen. He tells me how important it is to cleanse the fruits, and he shows me a fruit spray he's bought to cleanse it with. He wants me to watch as he sprays the apple until the dirt comes off. "See?" he says, and "Look, all the dirt is gone," and then he washes it repeatedly under cool water. He takes a clean knife, washes that, too, and slices the apple for me. He then washes the knife again and puts it in his place. "Taste," he says, as he brings the slice of the apple to my mouth. I take it and it is sweet, and cold. I acknowledge that it is a delicious apple, but I must go. He puts the apple slices in a sandwich bag for me and hands it to me. "For the road," he says, and our hands brush. I stare at him and remember. I remember holding him in his mother's kitchen, and telling him that he was the only man I could ever love, and I feel fortunate for having loved him, but luckier for having known when it was time to leave. I feel the lump in my throat loosening and I almost want to cry, but we smile instead and say goodbye.

As I am leaving, I hug his wife and kiss his daughter. My daughter holds on to him and promises to return. She hugs and kisses her sister and hugs the wife as well. I walk out and sigh as I hear the door close behind me. As we enter the elevator, my daughter speaks about what her father has bought her, the places they've been and what they've done. I listen to her as I exit the building and walk towards my present husband, who patiently stands in front of the car, waiting for us. I am relieved to be outside, taking in the warm air as I watch my husband come to me with a smile.

Waterloo

Jacob Appel

I've been dating Sally three months when she lobs me a *we need to talk*. We're sitting in the conference room at the Cedar Crest Bank, waiting for the Chamber of Commerce to discuss the contents of the time capsule. All around us the courtesans of local retail—barbershop aristocrats, service station gentry—are pushing themselves on the land developers and store-front attorneys who compose our municipal royalty. Sally's tie-dyed blouse and acid-washed jeans scream out against a graveyard of herringbones. This is where we first met (I deal in rare books and collectibles, she owns Hudson Valley Travel and Touring), but it's the last place I'd ever want to have an intimate conversation, especially one of those grappling *too-old-for-the-singles'-bars, please-don't-send-me-back-to-the-personals, but-things-seemed-to-be-going-so-well* exchanges that end in either fire or frost. At forty-one, I've already been dumped under my fair share of excruciating circumstances. On the observation platform at the Statue of Liberty. Between the his-and-hers coffins at Grant's Tomb. Even while chaperoning my nephew's senior prom. So I can't help wondering what I've done to deserve being streamlined under a cardboard sign pitching Roth IRAs?

"If this is the old heave-ho," I say, "can't we go where I can smoke a cigarette?"

Post break-up sex might be pressing too hard. A tobacco fix seems perfectly reasonable.

Sally steers me into the alcove behind the buffet table. Her scallop-shell necklace jingles as she walks. I survey the platters of complementary pastry, the apricot *hamantaschen* and brown-and-white cookies designed to win Morton's Deli a dispensation from the zoning commission, and I long to stuff Sally's mouth with pastries—to mute the tragic into the comic. Instead, I regress to break-up pose: hangdog, glasses in one hand, the other bracing my temple.

"No 'heaves' today," says Sally. "No 'hos' either."

"You had me worried there for a minute."

"You're always worried." Sally presses her fingers into my wrist. "When I *do* decide you're expendable, you'll have plenty of advance warning. Trust me. And don't hold your breath. But I'm glad I have you on the defensive, darling, because I'm about to raise the stakes."

Time to backpedal. I've already pulled a hat trick on divorces. Part of Sally's mystic allure is that she's loving me on somebody else's alimony. Why raise stakes? It'll just take longer to burn. I'd prefer to stake out a Third Way between marriage and bachelorhood. Something comfortable but not too committed. A page out of Willy Brandt. But if Sally doesn't see it that way, I fear, no woman ever will. This is a tête-à-tête I'd like to avoid.

"Let me guess," I say. "You've talked them into burying us together in the time capsule. A representative couple of the twentieth century."

"Better," says Sally. "I want to skip out on the time capsule entirely—"

"—And vacation in Tahiti?—"

"—And visit my family."

"You are kidding, aren't you?"

But Sally's eyes are as cold as marble.

One of the reasons I fell for Sally was that of all the childless women over forty I've met, she is the only one who doesn't waste her carpool energy on nonsense like theater outings and canasta socials and nieces' bridal showers. She wards off spinsterhood with vigor and civic responsibility. There are enough plaques on the walls of her office to make a dentist blush, and rumor has it that last Christmas she even rang a bronze bell for the Salvation Army. She's not a *guard-hearth-and-home-while-the-kids-are-away-at-college* kind of woman. Family talk makes me nervous.

"But I'm chairman of the committee," I say. "We've been planning this for months."

A millennium capsule in Cedar Crest Plaza. I'm hoping to win an achievement gavel.

"My sister's having a birthday party for her daughter. Up in Waterloo. We have to go."

"I didn't know your sister had a daughter," I say. "I didn't even know she was married."

I'm being honest. Her family is backdrop. I've never met any of them.

Sally shakes her head. "She's not married," she explains. "The guy knocked her up and hit the road. It's not something we talk about."

"And the daughter?"

"She choked to death," says Sally. "Five years ago."

This misfortune relaxes me. "So it's a memorial service?"

"No," says Sally, slapping her hands together and beaming false joy. "It's a birthday party!"

She scrounges through her purse and thrusts a pink envelope into my hand. I withdraw the invitation tentatively. Four clowns in a miniature blue convertible trail balloons across the page. They are asking us to celebrate the tenth anniversary of Tracy's birth. On the following Saturday. The printing is done in magic marker, each letter a different color. Rain or shine. RSVP. No indication that the child has gone the way of all flesh. I've heard all sorts of anecdotes from the Meade family album—about Sally's mother and the three-legged dogs, about her brother and his ongoing marriage contest—but this is too much. I look up for the punchline.

Sally squeezes my wrist again. All of the humor has petrified from her features. Behind her, the local potentates are milling about the coffee maker, bartering football scores and stock tips. We draw an occasional nod, maybe a smile. Nothing more. The time when our relationship provided grist for the gossip mill has long expired. We've earned our "couple-space."

"I'm not on *Candid Camera*?" I ask Sally, groping. "You're serious."

Sally smiles as though she's about to take a wet sponge in the face.

"She's my sister," she answers. "It's something she does."

~

On Saturday morning, we drive up the Hudson River to Waterloo. This is Washington Irving country, blueberry groves and yellow brick. The Meades rank among the provincial Wellingtons. They have been squandering fortunes in the Columbia Valley ever since Hezekiah Meade guzzled away a bonanza in Vermont granite. Sally's forebears are veritable alchemists: a pelt empire into jaundice, a lumber mint into cirrhosis of the liver. My family scrimps. Sally's fritters away. They take risks and we don't. We're even divided by the name of the town—my father taught European history, their village name, Waterloo, rhymes with stay-or-go—and I find myself wondering whether any amount of tenderness can surmount generations of slaughtered pronunciation. Maybe Sally was meant for a gambler from Vay-enna, Maine, or Mere-sells, Kentucky.

The back seat of the rental car is loaded high with gifts: Barbie accessories, Parker Brothers board games, a water raft shaped like a mermaid. But no marbles. No plastic figurines. Nothing capable of being ingested. We did a number on the poor salesclerk at Toy Paradise when we asked her to recommend presents equally suitable for a girl of four and a girl of nine—adding the caveat that they had to be larger than Sally's fist. The woman probably thought we'd been sent by the central office. Or a state agency. Some sort of quality control test. She pasted double bows on each of our purchases and carried them out to our car. That was when the full absurdity of this situation finally clobbered me—*we were buying birthday presents for a dead child!!!!!*—but what could I possibly say? It's Sally's family, not mine. Intervention betokens responsibility. Three marriages have taught me that if I try to straighten out Sally's sister, blow her perverse ritual to smithereens, it will only be a matter of time before I'm playing Atlas to all the Meades in Waterloo: Witnessing living wills; taking in orphaned children; carrying their emotional baggage on my back. Far better to hold my tongue and keep my distance.

We ride from the toy store to the county line in silence.

"You're awfully quiet," Sally finally says. "You're not happy about this."

"Peachy keen," I say. "I love birthday parties."

"Please, Ted. This is for me."

She shifts to the middle of the seat and glides her forearm across my abdomen. We haven't had sex all week—and when you don't live together, this feeds your insecurities—but I make a point of not responding. Sally reluctantly withdraws her arm.

"I don't expect you to understand," she says. "I don't even understand. Not completely."

She folds her arms across her chest. I fear she is crying, but I can't afford to look.

"Three hundred sixty-four days a year, Cynthia leads a normal life. She works. She pays her bills. She even dates on occasion. And she never talks about Tracy. Not since they released her from the institution. If she won't concede outright that the girl is dead, she also doesn't pretend she's alive. It's as though the child never even existed. But then November rolls around and we get another invitation....Will you please be kind to her, Ted? She's had such a hard life, and she's one of the sweetest people you'll ever meet."

It would be so easy to give away the kingdom. I change the subject.

"It's kind of funny, isn't it? You'd think that dating a travel agent would lead to all sorts of adventures, but the only place we've ever gone together is Waterloo—I mean *Waiter-low*, New York."

"Dammit, Ted! Don't be that way."

We cross the Bear Mountain Bridge and ascend into the Catskills. The narrow road winds its way along the river, as aimless as a summer breeze. I take comfort in the haphazard grades and random switchbacks. Or try to take comfort. Each of the women I've married has been like one of these roads. Free-spirited. Meandering. Tortuous. I've spent more than two decades of my life swerving to the twists and turns of women. The valleys continue to haunt me—the morning when I roped my first wife, my first ex-wife, into a futile attempt to retrieve my second, that empty night after my father's funeral when I phoned all three in reverse chronological order. Deep down I know that Sally is also like one of these mountain roads—but this time I've learned from past crashes. That's my comfort. I'm no longer afraid to drive into the embankment.

I look at my watch. "They're burying the time capsule now," I say.

"I don't want to fight," answers Sally. "Okay? Not today."

"Who's fighting? I was going to ask you what you would have put in it—I mean if you could put in absolutely *anything*. If you didn't need approval from the committee."

Sally shrugs. "I really don't know."
"Do you know what I'd put in?"
"What?"
"Abe Morton."
"Abe Morton from the deli???"
"You know why? Because they'd dig him out in thirty years and he still wouldn't have his dispensation."

Sally laughs. A floodgate laugh that laps and ripples for minutes. This is the first hint of joy she's shown since we left Cedar Crest, so I throw more municipal dignitaries into the time capsule. Big Thelma from Happy Housewares goes first; I wouldn't want to crush anyone. And how about Bernie Tillburn, the village attorney, who looks like an ostrich? Might as well keep his head in the sand. We pass the next hour preserving the Lions Club and the Ceder Crest Plaza Association for future generations. Sally's begging me to stop so that she can catch her breath. Her cheeks are scarlet. By the time I've exhausted all of the entrepreneurs worthy of mass burial and started in on ex-wives, tears are streaming down her cheeks. I'm wishing this moment could go on forever.

"Wait," says Sally. "Stop. You just drove past the house."

There are cars parked along the side of the road, but no traffic. I pull a three-point turn.

"Which house?" I ask.

Sally is still trying to compose herself.

"That one," she says. "Follow that dog."

It is a give-away, I'll admit: A three-legged Irish setter sporting a paper party hat.

~

We're the last of the guests to arrive and Sally's sister greets us at the door. Cynthia's body shows the wear of middle-age (an unkempt gray mane, rolling hips), but her attire is pure counterculture. Moccasins. A red bandanna tucked around her throat.

False gemstones adorning every finger. I've seen her thousands of times before: Sifting through bins of secondhand clothing on the streets of Provincetown and Woodstock, doling out unwanted assistance at New Age book shops. She's Sally's rustic alter-ego, I realize. This makes me instantaneously dislike her.

"I'm so *so* glad you could make it," says Cynthia. "And Tracy just *loves* her Aunt Sally."

Her voice registers somewhere between shrill and sing-song.

"We brought her presents," I say. "Big ones."

Sally grinds her heel into my foot.

"Tracy loves presents," answers Cynthia, oblivious. "And you must be Uncle Ted."

"Just Ted," I say, extending a hand.

Sally's sister responds with an embrace. She smothers me into her cleavage, presses her wet lips against my cheek. Her shampoo smells of earthenware. "Welcome to the family," she says. "Come meet everyone." Then she leads Sally and me—*both by the hand!*—into a musty den of wooly rugs and wicker.

I recognize all of the Meades from Sally's descriptions. The desiccated elderly couple sitting at either end of the loveseat are her Aunt Thelma and Uncle Max. Thelma's hair is dyed henna and puffed like meringue; her eyebrows are rainbowed in pencil. Max is a bulldog over a bow-tie. He sits grim and inert as though facing a firing squad. They've divorced and remarried each other three times. Standing at the bay window is Sally's mother, Edna, guardian of three-legged dogs. If she'd adopted the hapless beasts, I could forgive her. Even admire her. But she breeds them! There were two when Sally's father died and now there are nine. Nine dogs with twenty-seven legs between them. And then there is Sally's older brother, Charlie, the Lotto winner, his hand kneading the exposed thigh of a well-endowed blonde. He has been advertising himself on television for months: "Send in your photograph and marry a millionaire." I imagine that the blonde is the lucky winner.

I do not know the names of the dogs. I *do* know, by instinct, that Cynthia will introduce them first.

"Uncle Ted," says Sally's sister. "This is Rex. This is Bugle. This is Prowler."

"Enchanté," I say. I'm tempted to shake paws and topple them. Instead I lean into Sally's ear and whisper, "I suppose they save her a fortune on pedicures."

She glares at me and walks away.

I nuzzle the dogs behind the ears and shake hands all around. Uncle Max rolls his eyes at me, as if to warn me against what I'm getting into. Aunt Thelma pinches at my fingers at though they were a cherry pit. The blond woman, Lurleen, introduces herself as "One of the Three Finalists." The Meades could be the last six people on the planet with whom I'd want to celebrate anything. Except possibly liberation from confinement. I squeeze into the sofa between Sally and the blond woman and attempt to look inconspicuously at my watch. How long are we expected to wait, I wonder, before the dead girl opens her presents? How long before we go home?

The den is decked out with helium balloons and multi-colored streamers. A pin-the-tail-on-the-donkey poster is taped to the far wall. Loot bags sit in careful alignment on the coffee table. The set-up is far more lavish than anything I ever had as a kid. It is also stark-raving psychotic. My instincts tell me to unmask the charade, to announce that the child is dead. But I do nothing. If Uncle Max and Lurleen are willing to play along with this macabre ritual, who am I to object? They're as much outsiders as I am. The blonde certainly is. I'm watching her closely—she seems so composed—and then a wicked thought strikes me: Maybe she doesn't even know.

"One good thing," I whisper to Sally, "is that she can keep the streamers up all year long."

"Shhh!" she fires back. "She'll hear you."

So let her hear me, I want to say. Shout it from the rooftops.

Sally's sister distributes paper hats and noise makers. The hats are conical shaped as though designed for a party of dunces. There are rubber strings attached to hold them in place. Thelma adjusts her husband's and Lurleen snaps the cord into Charlie's chin. I can't help thinking of the safety instructions on airplanes: Be sure to put on your own oxygen mask before assisting your children. I refuse to be treated like a child and I balance the paper hat nonchalantly on my knee. Sally's mother glares at me. Her brother coughs. Reluctantly, I agree to blend in with the fools.

"Tracy should be here any minute," says Cynthia. "Let's turn off the lights and hide."

"A *surprise* party," I blurt out. "You can't be serious?"

"Tracy loves surprises," says Sally, emphasizing each word.

"I imagine *she* does," I say. "I guess I've outgrown them."

Edna Meade flicks off the lights and an unpleasant dusk settles over the room. The waning afternoon sun casts a rectangle from the bay window into the opposing plaster. The brother and his blonde, as if acting upon some Pavlovian trigger, practice cold fusion with their mouths. Sally pushes me roughly behind the sofa. Then her mother pulls the drapes and all is darkness.

Buried alive, I think. Like Abe Morton in the time capsule.

"On the count of three," whispers Cynthia. "Three...Two...One."

"Surprise!" they shouted.

The lights go on again. The noisemakers blare. I watch the Meades welcoming home their imaginary daughter, granddaughter, niece. I am surprised—surprised at the zeal of their cheering. Cynthia is bouncing and clapping like a contestant on a game show. Her mother and brother are puffing vigorously into paper snakes. Uncle Max bobs his head in approval. Even the dogs are yapping. Only Lurleen appears confused. Or possibly disappointed. But then the brother says something into her ear and she too is applauding.

"It's a good thing the girl's dead," I whisper to Sally, "Or she'd die of shock."

"Clap," she answers—angry. "Clap."

~

Sally's sister disappears into the kitchen and returns with a birthday cake. Chocolate frosting. Ten candles. *We Love You, Tracy* scrawled in pink calligraphy. Edna Meade croons the first bars of *Happy Birthday*, her voice high and scratchy like an old phonograph record, before the family joins in and drowns her out. I join in too. If I won't cheer for a dead girl, I can handle singing for my supper. Then Cynthia sets the cake on the coffee table. "Make a wish," she says. The flames shimmer in anticipation.

"Mission control," I whisper to Sally, "We have a problem."

We can't possibly be waiting for the flames to die from natural causes? Of course not. The Meades have been through this routine five times and each scene is meticulously choreographed. They have transformed dead girls' birthdays into in exact science. Edna Meade complains about the heat and Sally switches on the oscillating fan. The draught apparently stands in for the absent chill. Sally flicks the lever once again. And again. On. Off. On. The fan blades remain motionless. The cord is lodged only halfway into wall socket, but I must be the only one to notice this—and I say nothing.

"Damn it," says Sally. "It isn't working."

Discomfort settles over the room. Hot wax dribbles into icing.

"Ted," she says, approaching, "May I have a cigarette?"

"But you don't smoke."

"Give me a cigarette!"

She's quick on her feet, my Sally. She lights the cigarette with the candles and accidentally blows them out in the process. Or at least nine of them. She is already seated, coughing, when one stubborn flame returns to life. Like Lazarus, I think. Like the Phoenix. Decidedly not like Tracy Meade. All eyes focus on the offending candle. Cynthia paces between the coffee table and the bay window, wringing her hands. The blond woman crosses and uncrosses her legs. I'm still debating whether or not I should plug in the fan when Uncle Max produces a cigar from his breast pocket and douses the final flame.

"Happy birthday," chimes Edna. "Happy birthday."

"Can we open the presents?" asks the blonde. "We bought her a T-R-I-C-Y-C-L-E."

"First dessert," says Sally in a stern tone. "Then presents."

"That's right," echoes Cynthia. "First dessert, then presents."

Six years ago they did presents first and the birthday girl choked to death on the removable arm of an action figure. That's why Sally's sister blames herself. When she was in the institution, according to Sally, she had too much time to reflect. To rationalize. She decided the child ingested the toy because she was famished. Because they'd skipped lunch and put off dessert. So now she dishes out cake like Marie Antoinette. Dogs first, I can't help noting, then people. She still hasn't learned her lesson. Would she take a hint, I wonder, if I started gnawing at the gift-wrapped packages?

We eat the cake on paper plates with plastic cutlery. I'm served last. The delay gives me an opportunity to make my wish: I wish we could go home. I've been on good behavior so far, but tiptoeing on egg-shells makes me sarcastic. I'm always afraid of what I might say. Or maybe it's another matter entirely. Maybe the Meades remind me that there is a side to Sally that I'll never be able to reach: something colorfully outrageous, even otherworldly. I'm drawn to her spirit. Even charged by it. But around her family, I feel like the only flesh-and-blood actor in a cartoon universe.

"So how do you like Waterloo, Uncle Ted?" asks Charlie.

I can tell he's trying to be friendly, but I'm not in the mood.

"Nice enough place," I say. "Makes me feel like Napoleon."

"Ted!" warns Sally.

"I mean *Nay-pool-eean*."

"Ted!"

Sally kicks me under the coffee table. Hard.

"Why don't we tell a story?" Edna asks. "A family story."

"How about Great Grandpa Hezekiah and the granite quarry," suggests Thelma. "That's Max's favorite. Isn't it, Max?"

Max says nothing. He uses the candy dish as a spittoon.

"Tracy doesn't like that one," Cynthia objects. "Why don't we play a game instead?"

They argue back and forth for several minutes. Pleasing both the mute uncle and dead child seems impossible. He's too old for a round of Parcheesi, she's too young for Grandma Dorothy and the piano tuner. Impasse. I have a story of my own to suggest, *The Emperor's New Clothes*, but I am not ready to pay hell with Sally. I'd be happy to emulate Uncle Max, following in Lou Gehrig's footsteps, but Sally's brother has other ideas. Charlie seems hell-bent on conversation.

"So I hear you're working on a time capsule, Uncle Ted," he observes.

"Wow!" says the blonde. "That's awesome."

"It's not that big a deal."

"That's easy for you to say," she says. "I think it's amazing what science can do these days. I'm only a dental hygienist, but even in dentistry we've had some amazing advances. Instant imaging. Air-brush fillings. Of course, that's nothing compared to a time capsule. I've always wanted to go back and see my parent's wedding."

Finalist #3 is now in the spotlight. Floozie trumps stories and games.

"It's not a time *machine*, dear," says Sally, gently.

"Oh!" says Lurleen, dejected. "Too bad."

Sally presses me to explain the Cedar Crest Plaza Millennium Project. Uncle Max also takes an interest, leaning forward and cupping his ear, so I outline the master plan for the time capsule. I sound like a talking mission statement. The Meades don't seem to mind. When I enumerate the final contents—tickets from the commuter rail, best selling novels, etc.—the blonde woman starts 'oohing' and 'aahing.' Uncle Max slaps his thigh when I mention the photograph of Miss America. A contemporary beauty standard. Hotly debated. I neglect to mention Abe Morton and my ex-wives.

"So when are you burying it?" asks Cynthia. "Maybe we can all come down to watch."

"They buried it today," I answer. "We missed it for the party."

I could swear I hear Uncle Max mutter the word fool under his breath.

"Oh, well," says Edna. "Maybe in another thousand years, knock on wood."

"Well, I'm glad you came," says Cynthia. "It's always better to live in the present."

She laughs, a high-pitched chirping roll. I can feel myself about to veer into dangerous territory.

"I've never understood historians," she adds. "Preservation this, preservation that. We'd all be better off as a global community if we focused on the future. I have no objection to a time capsule, but don't you think the money might be better spent on saving the rain forests? Or feeding children?"

This is too much.

"Live ones or dead ones?"

My words strike like lightning. It is as though a collective rigor mortis sweeps across Sally's family, freezing them to cinder. Edna Meade's face turns the color of a bed sheet; Aunt Thelma's eyebrows rise into orbit. Charlie's fingers clench into the blonde's exposed thigh until she winces. Even Bugler cowers beside the table, shielding his eyes with his paw. Only Uncle Max exhibits any signs of life. He tucks his cigar is his between his lips and billows smoke. A faint smile curls the corners of his mouth. This is his way of thanking me, I can tell. His way of saying it's about time. But my solace is fleeting. I don't even have time to apologize. Cynthia heaves herself from the table and collapses, sobbing, against her mother's lap.

I turn to face Sally. She looks away.

"Ted and I are going outside to have a cigarette," she announces. "We'll be back."

~

We retreat onto the back veranda. I'd like to pretend that I am leading and Sally is following, but I sense her charcoal gaze prodding me forward. As though I were a wayward child or a pack animal. The undergrowth in the backyard is alive with the sounds of thrashers and mockingbirds. These are the dirges of twilight, I know, the knell of something ending. Sally walks slowly to the edge of the porch and gazes over the railing. I dust off a rocking chair—keeping my eyes on her back—and settle in with a squeak. Overhead, a wasp is trapped in the porch light, buzzing, throwing its tiny body against the dusty globe.

"How could you do that?" Sally asks. Her voice isn't angry,

but almost wistful. She's still not facing me, and her words seem directed at some wrong of the distant past. "How could you do that *to me*?"

"I'm sorry," I say. "It just happened."

"*What?*"

"She was talking about the time capsule and it just happened."

Sally shivers in the autumn chill. I long to hug her, but I don't dare. I know that I must make a decision, a decision whether to stay or go, and no amount of affection or even humor can come to my assistance. I have already given up my time capsule, sacrificed a large portion of my sanity. How much more absurdity can I endure before I risk becoming Uncle Max? And do I love Sally enough to find out? All I know for certain is that right now I want nothing more than to take her in my arms and blot out all of the Meades with their marriage contests and three-legged dogs and dead children's birthdays. To block out Waterloo.

I walk across the porch to Sally. She shakes off my embrace.

"It's all a big joke to you, isn't it? One big rip-roaring hilarious joke!"

"I'm sorry," I say again. "I just couldn't take it anymore. Can't we please go home?"

"*Go home? Now?* What you're going to do, Ted, is you're going to go back in there and pretend nothing ever happened. You're going to tell stories and you're going to sing and you're going to celebrate so hard that you're going to be genuinely disappointed when the party is over. Do you understand me? If she wants you to go upstairs and keep the kid company, you'll do it. If she wants you to teach the kid how to ride a tricycle, you'll do that too. Am I making myself clear? Because if you can't do that, Ted, *you* need to go home. Alone."

"Please, Sally...."

"Stay or go, Ted. Make your decision."

We're standing face to face, divided by shadow. From inside drift the sounds of renewed cheering and yelping dogs. How different things might have turned out if we'd stayed in Cedar Crest and buried the time capsule. If we'd avoided this bloodbath in Waterloo. But now we're here on the battlefield, and there's no turning back. We must either stay together or go alone. Stepping toward Sally, hoping to find wisdom in proximity, I see my answer in the stiff, weary features of a beautiful woman who has already grown old. Her face has survived the Meades. Nothing—not even my leaving—will age it any further. And somehow I know it is the face that will come to mirror mine, the face Sally will be wearing in thirty years when we are standing together, side by side, unearthing the time capsule.

"Let's go inside," I say.

Mision San Pablo

Steven Lewis

Here is what I do: I scan weeklies all over the state and hone in on some good family that for one reason or another catches my eye; it could be a photograph or a headline on the sports page or a couple of kids with the same last name on school honor rolls. Or none of those. The only thing that connects them is that they are complete strangers to me.

I drive to their town and observe them for several weeks; I see the kids waiting for the school bus in the morning. Some days I follow Mom to work. Some days, Dad. I go along with them to restaurants and movies. I mark down who mows the lawn — and when. I note when the lights go out each night. Eventually, I discern who is happy and who is putting up a front. I am only interested in the happy ones.

The job takes 45 minutes at most. I wait until the house is empty. Believe it or not, I often find an unlocked door and just walk in. If all doors are bolted, I simply tape and break a small pane of glass from a back door. (FYI, alarm systems are deal breakers.)

Their homes look like they are always expecting unexpected guests. Donning disposable rubber gloves and surgical shoe covers, I head straight to the parents' bedroom, clear each bureau top with a smooth Fred Astaire sweep of my arm, pull out the dresser drawers, rip and hang a pair of Mom's panties on the bedpost. Jewelry and prescriptions are thrown into a pillow case; the cash in Dad's sock drawer is stuffed in my back pocket. I then go about trashing the kids' rooms, shards of glass and ripped up posters and shattered computers piled on their beds, their names scribbled on the walls with mom's lipstick.

Down in the living room I knife the couch, rip family pictures off the walls, knock over the étagère, spear the flat screen with a fireplace poker. You can imagine the kitchen. Afterwards, I wash up in the bathroom, plug the sink and turn up the hot water.

For my time and effort I keep approximately 50% of the gross monies for food and rent and save the rest for the 22nd Mission Fund. The jewelry I take to the dump in a green plastic bag along with the rest of my daily trash. I'm not in it for the money.

*

Here's a bone: My father was a minister. We lived up in Butte County. I still see Father at the head of the maple table in his collar and ruddy cheeks, hands together and head bowed as he thanks the Lord for our daily bread. Mother sits to the right. She is wearing an apron. Five year-old Ruth sits across from me. I am seven. It is morning, the sun lighting up the daffodils Mama had put in the bay window.

The next thing I know Father's eyes are wide open like he'd seen the Devil himself and then he falls off his chair. The next thing I know we're living with my mother's parents in Fresno.

The tedious story of a childhood after a parent dies has been told and retold by so many other orphans that it seems pointless to make a point of it. Would you like to know that my grandfather died soon after of emphysema? That I found him in the backyard? That I tried and tried to be the good boy my mother said my father would want me to be? That my sister Ruth didn't try; at 15, she stole Gram's rainy day money and ran off with 22-year-old Ray Don Walton?

Well, believe any or all of it, if you must. But my intent is not to leave subtle psychological clues alongside the path of this narrative so that shortly after the climax you will smile, nod gravely or raise your finger as if you truly understand. This is not about pathology. I will not allow you that easy consolation.

Instead, I offer you the story of the Jostens, my grandparents' next door neighbors. They befriended me and Gram after Ruthie disappeared and my mom drowned herself in a bottle. (I neglected to mention that.)

So a decade after we fled Paradise for Fresno, I was sitting in Gram's yellowed kitchen with the Jostens eating a white Ralph's sheet cake with a chocolate mortarboard and tassel on top. Mrs. Josten's thick lower lip trembled as she held out a forkful of cake, saying she was so proud that I would be going to the seminary in the fall. Then Mr. Josten, a high school teacher and deacon at the Methodist church, got up from his chair, walked around behind me and laid his thick pink hand on the back of my skinny neck. I bowed my head. "Paul," he said, "each of us has something special to give to others. It is God's plan. Because you have known so much unhappiness in your young life, I think you may have more to offer than many others. Look around and see who needs you."

I dutifully lifted my head against the weight of his moist palm and twisted around. "Your father," he continued, "named you Paul for good reason, Paul. Heed well the words of your namesake: 'Take pleasure in infirmities, in reproaches, in necessities, in distresses for Christ's sake: for when you are weak, then are you strong.'"

I stared at the closed eyes of a man who wouldn't recognize real distress if it smacked him across his boneless face. He saw Jesus, but did not see the cross.

So that night while they were at church, I ransacked the Josten's lovely colonial home, unsettling their earthly lives forever. And over the ensuing eight years, through seminary training and beyond, I made it my mission to toss similarly weak, narcissistic souls into maelstroms of confusion and despair — and in the process help them to save their eternal souls.

*

In retrospect, my problem is that I am weak. After eight thankless years, maybe I got bored — or perhaps ambitious. Certainly, I was insulted. Maybe all three.

My undoing began with the Weiners' uncanny ability to bounce back from adversity. It was always my practice to hang around for a few weeks to observe the results of my charity, but within a mere ten days of my intrusion into their homey home near Gilroy, the Weiners had seemingly returned to normal. The resolutely thin Mr. and Mrs. lost only a day at their respective jobs; the three kids, Jennifer, 17, Sarah, 15, and Benjamin, 13, never even skipped school.

Workmen were at the site by day two to repair the damage that the family was unable to clean up themselves. And at 14 days, when I should have been packing, they were no longer locking the house in the morning.

So I bided my time and returned to their split-level fortress 40 days after my first incursion. The place looked like I had never been there. I methodically went over some of the same old territory — Mrs. W's pink lace underwear, the diaphragm, the posters, the couch, the family photos — just to let them know it was me, and then upped the ante: I slipped the dead robin I had found in the backyard beneath their comforter. I hung Benjamin's bobble head Barry Bonds doll by the neck from the ceiling. I trashed Jennifer's room and wrote "Lightning Strikes Twice" on her mirror. The coup de grace, however, was leaving Sarah's room absolutely untouched.

When I returned to the neighborhood a few days later to make sure my mission was finally accomplished, I was heartened by the sight of an expensive alarm system. Better still, on Saturday after I tailed the good doctor and his handy friend, Ray, to Ace Hardware to buy motion sensors, I heard him mutter, "Barb is devastated!" And when he whispered through the side of his mouth, "I can't even comfort her," Ray and I understood that there was no sex going on at 9 Arbor Lane.

Yet something continued to gnaw at me. I was irked by how quickly they had reassembled the second time. It took the Sadowskis from Sonoma three months just to get a new sofa. And when I saw the "For Sale" sign in the Weiners' front yard, I almost became unglued. Did they think they could escape me? The arrogance of that family was appalling.

A week later, by mere chance (as if ...), I was driving through the neighborhood early one morning and got stopped behind the school bus in front of their house. Jennifer came running out and gestured with one finger to the driver. Then she walked directly at my car, veering off at the curb and stepping into a van behind me. Thirty seconds later, Dr. and Mrs. Weiner appeared on the small porch, followed by Sarah. She kissed both of her parents and ran to the bus.

They turned and spoke to the darkness in the door. Benjamin, 13, was staying home; probably a cold or the flu. I imagined— yeah, I knew — what mom and dad said to do if someone came to the front door.

I also knew he wouldn't listen. An hour after the parents left, I parked a few blocks away and knocked on the front door. Benjamin peeked out from behind a slit in the new drapes and by the time he turned the knob on the front door I had the stocking over my head and rammed the door open, pushing him backward toward the stairs.

I screamed that I'd kill him if he didn't listen to everything I said. And when he started to cry, crumpled up on the steps, I kicked him in the meaty part of his thigh and, jabbing him from behind, shouted "UP THE STAIRS! IN YOUR ROOM! IN YOUR ROOM!", shoved him onto the bed and tied him to the headboard with rope I had in my pocket. I cut it with a knife and gagged him with a strip of sheet I ripped out from beneath him. Wide-eyed, he urinated in his pajamas.

Let me assure you — in case you, in your presumptive wisdom, think we're headed down mutilation highway — I was not going to hurt the boy. That is not my mission. I wasn't even interested in trashing the place again. I merely emptied Mrs. W's jewelry box into the toilet and, upon finding a box of blank checks in Dr. W's desk drawer, just tore out one check in the middle of a book. That was it. A gesture.

Then I went into Sarah's room, as I knew I would. The room smelled of scented candles. The bed was made. Ironed and folded clothing was stacked in a laundry basket. On her night table, resting on top of the unopened book, was a Doors CD, Ruth's favorite when she was a teenager. I plopped down on the neat bedspread — certain to leave an impression — and then slipped the CD into my jacket pocket and went downstairs. There was nothing else to be done.

As I reached the front door, however, the phone rang. I picked it up – thoughtlessly? arrogantly? -- a woman's voice, "Hello. . . . hello?. . . . Ben, are you there. . . . ?" I replaced the receiver. At the time it seemed like a nice touch.

I quickly yanked off the stocking, peeled the gloves from my sweaty hands, folded it all into my pocket and walked out the door, bumping right into Jennifer and a tall boy with long stringy black hair.

I recognized him as a clerk at the 7-Eleven directly across from Hotel 6 ("Weekly Rates") across town. We never spoke — he doesn't interest me — but it was his thin fingers into which I had passed a lot of the Weiners' cash. The terror in Jennifer's eyes as she stepped backward bore a family resemblance to Benjamin. "Who are you?" she gasped, grasping the boy's bare arm.

I glared directly through the maelstrom into her green eyes. "I'm the assessor; just counting rooms for the tax rolls ... shouldn't you be in school, Jennifer?"

She was unable to speak, her lips barely parted. The phone rang again. She looked up — as if to ask permission — and then rushed around me, knocking my shoulder and racing through the open doorway. The lanky boy stood there, though, studying my face from behind those dark, bony antediluvian sockets, a bewildered animal peering into a dark cave. I pushed him aside and walked out the door.

"Heeeeeeeeey! I know you!" I suddenly heard behind me. I never turned around, walking down the driveway and onto the sidewalk as if I didn't hear him.

"Heeeeeeeeey!" I felt him running at my back and started to race. I had wings. By the time I was three blocks away I heard the whining sirens and turned my head to find my pursuer. The kid was nowhere. Like a dog, he must have stopped at the first corner. No oxygen. No vision. Just going through the motions like everyone else.

But, of course, he'd be the one to tell the police where I lived.

I stood there panting, leaning on a telephone pole as if it was my staff. And when I was sure that no one was around, I slipped behind a tall hedge, removed the sport coat, folded it inside out the way Mr. Josten taught me to do years ago, walked down another block and a half to the car, keyed the trunk, opened the suitcase, laid the coat neatly across the rest of my clothes, examined the CD and then put it back. I chose a mustache and glasses from my case the way mother used to choose earrings from the top of the dresser, rolled my sleeves and shut the lid. Pressed down on the trunk. The engine turned over right away and I drove all day and through the night to this next godforsaken town where they probably wouldn't know God if He opened up a MacDonald's.

Tomorrow will be time enough to decide where to keep pursuing my mission. It doesn't much matter, you know. People are the same all over. The fact that I almost got caught reminds me only that I am not infallible. I am not God. That is why I write this down. I offer you the Weiners as proof of my contemptible weakness, my growing strength. That is all.

That is all.

I know you hear me. I know you want this story to go somewhere you recognize. You want me to get caught, to fall in love, to be reborn in Christ, to be writing this from some mental institution like that fool Holden Caulfield.

I know you better than you know yourself. I know where you live. Some of you even want me to contact Ruth. Whatever. You would even be satisfied if I returned to kill the Jostens or Benjamin or Jennifer or the tall lanky boy. (His name is Jerry.)

Don't be naive.

Raised Hearts Hailing:
The Poems of Francis Eamon Boyle (1874-1900)

William Boyle

I overheard a curious snatch of conversation at one of the weekly socials that are run at Club Cruiskeen. A pretty golden little baggage was talking to her lover.

"D'you know, Godfrey, only last night I learnt many interesting things about my family. D'you know that my great-grandfather was killed at Waterloo?"

"Rayully, sweetness, which platform?"

The golden head was tossed in disdain.

"How ridiculous you are, Godfrey. As if it mattered which platform."

Naturally, I cannot guarantee that this couple said these words or even opened their beaks at all. The room was full of my Escorts.

— Myles na Gopaleen
(Flann O'Brien)

And if, as you claim, I only imagined them, what was the crime in that? They were so beautiful.

— Sir Edmund Roberts

My paternal great-grandfather, the poet Francis Eamon Boyle, lived to see only seven of his poems published, by a small Dublin press in the fall of 1898. The poems were printed, like Myles na Gopaleen's famous "Scorn for Taurus," in eight-point Caslon on turkey-shutter paper with covers in green corduroy. The original title of the book, Francis's title for it, *I Was Pissed When I Wrote These Lines*, was rejected and the book was published as *Seven Poems of Deep Sorrow* in a limited edition of three hundred copies. Francis's signature was scrawled across the first page above the first poem, "The Death of Robert Griffiths." Since Francis's handwriting was very poor, though, to the untrained eye, to the not-Boyle, the signature resembled something that I can only guess looked like a quatrefoil run through with gigantic spikes or a swollen ram's skull decorated with hollow half-grapefruits and mangled shoehorns. The tragic, drunken signature added to the overall sorrow of the poems.

Thomas Farrell, Francis's drinking buddy and biographer, notes that, of the seven poems that appeared in the book, Francis had written six (with the exception of the final poem, "Another Night Fell") in one evening, less than a week before the book went to press, fueled by a night of boozing at Lyle Standish's pub in Corkadoragha that included fifteen pints of Guinness and twelve shots of Powers whiskey. The book was a minor success. About a hundred copies were sold across Ireland (most people, it has been said, did away with the green corduroy cover) and my great-grandfather was spoken of as a poet of great ambition and humor with a promising future. It was said that William Butler Yeats and Lady Augusta Gregory regarded the book as one of the finest of the time, and both longed to make acquaintance with the poet. Thomas Farrell, who later befriended both Yeats and Lady Gregory, writes that their fascination with my great-grandfather faded quickly and that after reading the tiny book of Francis's and expressing some interest in meeting him, he seemed to go out of their heads until all they remembered of him was that he was something of an oddity. Yeats, Farrell writes, when questioned in 1901 about the importance of Francis Eamon Boyle, said, "Oh yes, the fellow whose book was wrapped in green corduroy. Honestly, all I remember now is that dreadful cover" (Farrell 212).

In 1899, Francis met my great-grandmother, Jean McClafferty—"A hell of a wicked woman," he later admitted to his friend John Barnard—was married, settled down, and began a family. Thomas Farrell notes:

In the first months of his marriage, Boyle worked almost constantly. He wrote four or five poems a day and seemed to be very content, waking early and working late into the evening. He was sober for a change and that had quite an interesting effect on his poems: Instead of writing about drinking strong liquor, losing his shoes, and hollering at his maiden the moon, he turned to writing devotional poetry, what he called "poems for Our Lord, Heaven Bless Him." (31)

In the summer of 1900, however, at the peak of his talent, Francis developed pneumonia, and spent the final two months of his life in a hospital bed. He died a week after his and Jean's first child, my grandfather Denis, was born. He left behind, in a beat-up old trunk, an impressive collection of writing: finished poems, notes for poems, prayers, and two stories (not to mention ten unopened quarts of Powers whiskey).

In 1908, the young poet M. Devlin discovered a tattered copy of *Seven Poems of Deep Sorrow* at a bookstore in Connemarra (he too did away with the green corduroy cover) and attempted to track down the author. His trail led him to Jean and eight-year-old Denis, who introduced him to Francis's "vaults." Devlin, awed by the amount of whiskey and paper that could be crammed into so small a trunk, found material enough for two more books, *My Fortune Yours* and *Raised Hearts Hailing*, both published in 1909 by Devlin himself on corrugated onion skin in twelve-point

Pepista Centaura (a type used in prison documents at the time). Calvin Rourke, in his 1923 *Introduction to Little Known Irish Poets*, which includes chapters on both M. Devlin and my great-grandfather, wrote that Devlin's discovery that day was both a disaster and a blessing. It was a disaster because Devlin filched the whiskey that he found, stayed drunk for the better part of a year and, sadly, never wrote another worthwhile verse himself. The writing of Francis Boyle's that he found, however, and managed, in his drunkenness, to publish, allowed us invaluable insight into the mind of a neglected genius who, if he was good at poetry when he was drunk (see *Seven Poems of Deep Sorrow*), was even better at it, it seemed, married and sober. (Rourke 217)

Rourke had very little else of interest to say about my great-grandfather, but his publication (it also had a cover of green corduroy) was a major boost to Francis's reputation, and soon *Raised Hearts Hailing* and *My Fortune Yours* were in wide circulation.

Francis's revival had a tremendous impact in particular on Irish poets of the 1920s and '30s. Poets like Brian Murray, Mairéad McMenemy, and William Finian praised and imitated Francis, declaring that he was Irish poetry's only indispensable voice. Finian, in 1925, dedicated an entire book of poems, *I Say Little Hunger*, to his "master, Francis Boyle," and modeled each poem after a poem of Francis's (Finian 2). The title, in fact, is taken from Francis's poem "Promontory," which begins: "I say village hunger, / I say little hunger. / I leave prayers on your holy head." Francis's influence was not constrained, however, to Ireland. It was, quite on the contrary, far-reaching. The Russian poet Vladimir Mayakovsky, in 1925, five years before he committed suicide, cited, in an interview with R. B. Garrett in *DFC Magazine*, Francis as one of his major sources of inspiration. "I keep the lines from his 'Lament for Mabel O'Connell'–'The woman wails / The dog howls / The twilight is happening now'–above my writing desk," Mayakovsky said (Farrell 376). The American poet Robinson Jeffers also credited Francis as an early great influence on him. Jeffers, interviewed by Thomas Farrell in 1930, said that "[w]ithout the example of Francis Boyle, I might not have written poems like 'To the Stone-Cutters' and 'Continent's End.' Boyle was a master: furious, elegiac, and extraordinary" (316). And Francis's poems, especially those written in his end-of-life fit of sobriety and published posthumously, are just that: furious, elegiac, extraordinary. He bears much in common with his contemporaries: Yeats, J. M. Synge, and more closely, Thomas MacDonagh and Seamus O'Sullivan. But he owes his greatest debt in this matter, it seems, to Irish Song. The songs that Francis knew, loved, and sang, he often said to Thomas Farrell, had the ability to capture the sadness and loveliness of life and love (something poetry, he added, was often incapable of because of its entanglements with pride), and they were the best way, he felt, to praise both Ireland and the Lord. Songs, he said, "could be mournful and cheerful and they required nothing but an extension of heart and a closing of the eyes, and they gave back all the knowledge of rain" (475). As a result, Francis often modeled poems after songs. "Woeful Rosaleen," for instance, borrows its refrain from Edward Walsh's version of "Have You Been at Carrick." "Autumn Visit" from *Raised Hearts Hailing* is a direct descendant of Eugene O'Curry's version of "Do You Remember That Night." "Peggy O'Leary" and "The Devil's White Beard" from *Seven Poems of Deep Sorrow* are both derived from the Anglo-Irish ballad "Colleen Rue." And "My Breeches Is Stole, My Pipe It Is Broke," also included in *Seven Poems*, lifts its title from a line in Hugh MacGowran's "O'Rourke's Feast." In "My Fortune Yours," arguably Francis's most famous and noteworthy poem, he writes a sort of love song for Song:

Stiffened words leave nightmares: a murder of crows in the throat, a crumbling statue that weeps whiskey, a bone to close the eyes. But Song—oh Song!—leaves God's signature on my tongue and heart.

Thomas Farrell calls Francis "a profound mystical thinker. His thoughts on song—his equation of song with rain-knowledge—and his exclamation that song was the finest expression of God-love and native land-love, places him, I think, amongst the most important thinkers anywhere in the last two hundred years" (645). Farrell goes on to discuss my forebear's significance as a religious poet: "The religious fervor of his poems recalls that of Saint John of the Cross. Francis Boyle redefined man's relationship with God in a way that people understood" (658). In Francis's world there was room for despair, but the despair was really love-longing, and the love-longing was for God. In Enniskerry, where he lived with Jean, Francis had the reputation of a priest, and his poems, which he showed often to friends and family, held the weight of homilies.

Francis was also an innovator of language. His final poems, the twelve that he wrote on his deathbed, published as the final book of *Raised Hearts Hailing*, are his most puzzling and venturesome. Samuel Briar, in *The Outcast and The Moon*, calls them "his final Act, his *Wake*, his soliloquy with Death, his attempt to understand a journey of spasmodic coughing and sweat-deadness" (242). Francis wrote the poems in pencil on cloth napkins, an arduous task. Having been offered a pad by his nurse, he refused, saying that his last poems *had* to be on cloth. When done, he requested that Jean neatly fold each napkin and place them in order of composition at the bottom of his trunk. M. Devlin, upon discovering them years later, was pleasantly surprised and baffled by the decade-old napkin-poems. It was great work on Devlin's part to decipher Francis's handwriting, which, with death haunting the poet, was, according to Devlin, "even worse than usual. It was as if he had tried to murder the napkins with slow, deliberate strokes. The—what I can only call 'pencil etchings'—looked like men losing their minds. They looked like bird droppings slaughtered with a hammer. I would not hesitate to say that they resembled the devil's vomit" (Farrell 415). Though puzzling, the poems are no doubt among Francis's finest work. Devlin was correct in thinking that they would make a fine ending to the second collection. The poems are not titled. Each begins with a brief quote from the Book of Psalms and a drawing of a box (or coffin, as Thomas Farrell has posited), and they are written without punctuation and with random capitalization and word-connection, yet they are in no way careless. The final poem, "Twelve" as it has come to be called, the most bizarre of all and the briefest, reads:

my Life is all morningthismorning and Great God birds
My life used to be the dawn Surprisedwhiskey and strangeness Oh I lost the morningtothemorning I lost it
When oh when in dark night did I lose it What foul lang-uage am I seeking ohIseekitsure my Lord I seek it

Thomas Farrell suggests that the poems are Francis's attempt at creating a death-language. Francis, he writes, "saw dying as a journey towards the Lord, the only way to reckon it being in a mad language, a language that sounded like bleeding and suffering, that looked like a bone breaking or a heart slowing down. The texture of Francis's final poems is exact: Words are mutable and delicious. Francis's torment is Apostolic, his unquiet revelatory" (514). If Francis's last poems are, as Farrell proposes, an attempt to undress the language of death and dying, then Francis, all the while, is the middle life's regardful supplicant. In the eleventh deathbed poem he lays claim to such a position:

Stranglethroated witness I am to languagestrangled

I kneel and receive alms oh Lord watch the strangledrivers-flow

Thus, Francis's poems never seek to discover and explode death's mysterious language (a language of crossing, of being handled), but to delight in its unexplainableness.

My grandfather Denis, before he died in 1988, told me quite a bit about Francis. He read me his poems (even the deathbed ones) at a very young age and often said that Francis was a trumpeter. He always called him that: a trumpeter. When I would ask him what he meant by it, he would smile and say, "A decoder, a great singer, an angel of the Lord." It got to be a routine with us. When I was fifteen, seven years after my grandfather's death, I began to read Francis's poems in a different way. They began to affect me. I found a rare book dealer in the city and bought a copy of *Seven Poems of Deep Sorrow*. My grandfather had left me with one, but I somehow needed my own. The green corduroy cover had long ago been removed but the turkey-shutter paper was in good shape, and the Caslon type smelled fresh. I read the seven poems about drunkenness, about wild boys like wild dogs running by the River Liffey, about youth and how it goes, about Francis the Moon-Hollerer on dark blessed nights and how the Irish moon of a hundred years ago sang to him and told riddles. I read the poems and I was alive. I was drunk with my great-grandfather at Lyle Standish's Corkadoragha pub. I stood by his side and wept and then I was him weeping and then I was my grandfather weeping and then we were separate again and we were all weeping, a trinity of weepers. It was powerful really reading those poems for the first time. I found my grandfather's copies of *My Fortune Yours* and *Raised Hearts Hailing* and read and reread them with the same voracity. I realized that Francis was a poet unlike any other. I understood what my grandfather meant when he called him a "trumpeter" and a "decoder." From Francis's poems one could extract faith and song. I will end now with lines of Francis's from "With Cormac, at Montague's Boat," a poem included in *Raised Hearts Hailing,* that I hold most dear:

I wept and knelt at the hundredth moonlight,
Cormac, raw and drunk at my side.
I wept a thousand widenesses, and thorns,
and I heard the music from the Lord's window.
I was wide and alive and I ached to lift my heart.

Works Consulted

Boyle, Francis Eamon. *Seven Poems of Deep Sorrow.* Dublin: Tiny Pennies Press, 1898.
---. *My Fortune Yours.* Dublin: Red Branch Press, 1909.
---. *Raised Hearts Hailing.* Dublin: Red Branch Press, 1909.
Briar, Samuel. *The Outcast and the Moon.* New York: The MacMillan Company, 1938.
Farrell, Thomas. *A Raised Heart: The Life and Poems of Francis Eamon Boyle.* London: Faber & Faber, 1929.
Finian, William. *I Say Little Hunger.* Dublin: Royal Irish Academy, 1925.
Kline, Robert. *The Forgotten Voyage of the H.M.S. Baci: Sir Edmund Robert's Quest For Sea Maidens and Sea Masters in the Seven Seas of the Explored World.* Volume One. St. Augustine: RK Books, 2001.
Montague, John. *The Book of Irish Verse: Irish Poetry from the Sixth Century to the Present.* New York: Bristol Park Books, 1998.

O'Brien, Flann. *The Best of Myles na Gopaleen.* New York: Penguin, 1983.
Rourke, Calvin. *Introduction to Little Known Irish Poets.* London: Hogarth Press, 1923.

A Supermarket In Upstate New York
Shadowing Allen Ginsberg

Barbara Adams

Cashiers and Packers

Felicia wears a used mink jacket, especially when she's near the door, her name tag pinned to the *ShopnSave* dark green shirt underneath her mink jacket stretched over her swollen belly, but she can't sit down like supermarket cashiers I've seen in Europe. But she smiles all the time at no one.

Judy puts canned corn peas Campbell's soup soda bottles beef chicken apples oranges frozen dinners ice cream milk Bud six-pack in *ShopnSave* plastic bags careful not to make them too heavy. Ringed with false black eyelashes on upper and lower lids like a raccoon, her hazel eyes are slightly crossed. *ShopnSave* hired Judy from the agency for the intellectually challenged so she is not allowed to run the computerized cash register. Do you have to be literate to scan cans?

Denise has worn a splint on her wrist and forearm for a year as she lifts the heavy shopping bags into my cart. I say Thank You and she goes blank, open-mouthed, her deep brown eyes and dark curly hair offsetting crooked, pegged teeth and I finally realize why she never says Hello when she passes my house walking a fat friendly beagle, because she has been warned not to talk to strangers.

Cart Retriever, Floor Mopper

Stanley pushes his wheeled pail and mop to a puddle of vinegar and pickles from a jar, sweeps the glass into a dustpan and dumps it into a garbage bag squeezes the mop from the pail of gray disinfectant wipes up the vinegar squeezes the mop again swishing it until the floor is clean and smells like pine then wheels mop and pail towards the back passing me as I look for a particular brand of canned tomatoes. "Can I help you?" Stanley asks, his name on a badge pinned to his clean green *ShopnSave* shirt like Judy and Felicia he was hired by the same agency as Judy and Denise dropping his mop beckoning me to follow him "There!" he points, so happy I think he will dance like Fred Astaire out to the parking lot to gather up carts like stray cats.

Deli Counter Server

Angela slices ham on the treacherous electric machine her hand in plastic glove an inch from the whirring blade. "That thin enough? Here," she says holding up a slice of ham and I eat it like a child getting a free lollipop. Pink paper numbers held hopefully like lottery tickets in customers' hands "Sixty? Sixty-one? Sixty-two?" she hits the button to advance numbers on a red digital sign and a fat mother with two small children in the cart yells "Bingo!" triumphantly. "A pound of baloney a pound of American cheese a pound of turkey on sale—sliced thin!" Angela unwraps the fat pink baloney slices wraps it unwraps cheese slices wraps it unwraps turkey slices it wraps it weighs packs "Sixty-four? Sixty-five?" Until "00" and her break to pee and smoke two cigarettes her *ShopnSave* green cap turned sideways like a rap artist atop her frizzy brown hair and goes back to the deli "Have a nice day!" laughing with toothless gums wide open.

Flower Girl

Rosa wraps my bouquet of roses in pink tissue paper with white curly ribbon ringing up the charge 3/$12 for assorted colors—red, golden, white fringed with magenta—adding tax to scentless flowers grown in Colombia thorns stripped off by young black-haired women chilled in cartons like small coffins shipped to *ShopnSave* for $5 a dozen the Columbian women get one dollar for ten dozen de-thorned bouquets meaning I paid them somehow. "Taxes!" Rosa screams. "I'll have to sell my house teachers are paid like queens work 5 hours a day don't work summers I'd love to have summers off where will I get the money this time?"

Shoppers

Old Man with merry dark eyes wearing a tweed cap touches his fingers to the edge of the brim as we pass. "It's cold." Not as cold as last winter. Much colder then. Yes. He heads down the aisle one way I the other. We cross paths again in the next aisle of paperback books romance mystery self-help bestsellers remaindered cooking reading titles and we smile like old friends as I check to see if he's wearing a wedding ring and is but I lost mine in the ocean.

An Older Old Man in a light tan raincoat and brimmed hat trundles along behind his purposeful wife grey curls tight as corkscrews picking out the cheapest brands of canned corn and peas pushing the shopping cart like a battering ram filled with armanent—Metamucil Fixodent Immodium Milk of Magnesia—asking her weary husband what he wants for dinner as he pulls his shaking right hand out of his coat pocket and an airline-size bottle of whiskey falls to the floor rolling towards my foot and I reach for it but he bends stiffly and puts it back in his pocket before his wife turns around.

Sick Shoppers

Elderly woman leaning on a walker after waiting for twenty minutes struggles to the Pharmacy counter a plastic tube feeding oxygen into her nostrils, pink plastic pocketbook dangling from her fat white arm, a little girl with long black hair holding onto the walker as the pharmacist in white coat with a label that says "Chi Abalalla" shakes his head "Medicare won't pay for this" he says as the elderly woman gasps for breath and looks at the little girl who translates into Spanish and the pharmacist tells her to call Medicare or she'll have to pay $293.38 she opens her pink plastic purse snaps open a change purse and shows him a $20 bill "Take" she says and the pharmacist takes her $20 bill and gives her ten pills to tide her over until Medicare turns her down.

I give Chi my name and he goes to the filing drawer marked A and pulls out a white paper bag with the refill prescription stapled to it, repeats my name, I nod, sign my name on the computer screen and hand over a $20 bill, my insurance co-pay. I leave the supermarket, get in my car and look at the label on the prescription bag and see my name but not my address and it's a prescription for birth control pills. Back to the pharmacy Pat who used to own her own drugstore is on duty smiles and says "Hi, how are you Barb?" and I show her the prescription with the wrong address and Pat says "This is not good we're supposed to check birthdates" taking it to show Chi who peeks out and studies a woman clearly beyond the need for birth control and Pat goes to the A file and finds another prescription with my name and my address. When I get home I take a pill and wonder if the other Barbara had taken my pills would she have felt better. Or just got pregnant.

Hell On Earth; Heaven Comes; Give Peace A Chance

Abigail Robin

So what that I took some money from some strangers. I have an excuse. Not like the rest of humanity.

I'm bi-polar according to the experts, who can't even make the necessary distinctions between shoe polish and shit. Those experts. They're certain that they know how all the parts of the brain and the genetic make-up determine a kid's emotions, moods, and behavior. Those doctors stuff little kids with drugs when the parents complain that the teacher can't control the little tike's behavior in school. Schools are prisons. What little kid needs to be in a prison?

I don't know how I got to this place or any other hospital or jail from San Diego to Bend, Oregon, Nashville, Tennessee, and back to the Hudson Valley, where I grew crooked. I useta live in wide-open spaces. I got caught in the mental health net, and now all I see are barred windows, frail-bellied trembling young boys, fat-bellied guys leaning against vomit green walls. We, the patients, wait for the three-ounce pill cup carried by some hip nurse wearing overalls. I even have enough patience to wait for the cute chick to bring the panacea to cut out the sound of keys jangling and locks turning in two-inch silver plated aluminum cylinders. In jail they make you wear these orange jump suits, and if you go out of the prison, they shackle you.

I guess I know how I got here. You see, there was this black and white racing car with a red light flashing that brought me here. I mean those drivers nearly caused three accidents rushing through red lights and stop signs just to snare me. I got picked up on the San Diego Freeway. The freeway is a free place, right? I wanted to protest; so I did. I attached an American Flag to this here gnarled wooden walking stick, and I planted myself in the middle of the freeway. Ya see, I was regressing to some past life. Like man, I was Davy Crocket, Sam Houston, and Andrew Jackson all rolled into one, stonewalling my way to reality. I was saving the Indians' great land from the destruction of the white men and their phony advertising slogans. JUST DO IT! So I did it and look where it landed me! I screamed, waving the flag, the symbol of democracy.

Emet is truth in Hebrew. I've always been so confused about language and religion. What do they really mean? Do they tell us what the truth is? I mean what we mean to say, what we say without being mean, what we mean to do is so confusing. Words seem to hurt more than bullets, than knives. Words are kisses of death or life. I'm not quite sure. And that's where that fucking advertising comes in. I mean, just because some TV ad tells us we can fly, we go out and try. I mean look at Icarus. He flew too close to the sun; he was the son of a father who gave him wings. I mean if someone gives you something, you go with it. Right! I mean you just don't sit on your ass wondering about getting more. I mean you do something with what you have. God bless America the land of RAGE and the home of the CAGE.

I remember my mother telling me this story of some woman flying out of her six-story window in the Bronx. My mother was six years old. She saw this flying form go by the window and she heard a splat. One thing about my mother is that she can always tell some kinda disaster story. She's got this, what they call an ironic sense of things. There's always a shadow encircling her. Not only that, but she has to try every psychological therapy in the new age arena. I was sixteen when she dragged me off to The EST Training. Maybe, that's when the trouble started. I mean that so-called damn training made me crazy. I mean I had to stand in front of all those people and tell them I was scared shitless. I mean, what kinda teenager wants to admit he's scared shitless? It seemed that when I did that training, there was somethin else going on. Maybe it was that I realized I was mortal. After that, I quit baseball and track; my grades tumbled like a thirty-story building on a fault-line. That myth of Sisyphus got me. Here I was having great success, and I quit! Ya know those Romans and Greek myths? They can really fuck you up. The truth is, life can fuck you up. Ya think you got it, and then all of a sudden, it disappears.

Ya know, I know my story sounds kinda confused. I mean the time is all screwed up. I got the San Diego Psychiatric Center confused with the Hudson River Psychiatric Center. I feel all mixed up. I mean, I was in so many places, hospitals, group homes, and jails in such a short time that I didn't even know that my head was attached to my neck, and that my neck was attached to my chest and that my heel bone was connected to my thigh bone. I mean, I was not anywhere to be found in my body. And ya know sumthin, you gotta know where your body is or else it's all over!

On one of my maniac episodes, I went down to Nashville. Abatollah, my mother, didn't believe me when I told her that Johnny Cash came to bail me out of the Nashville jail. Here I was performing at the Grand Olde Oprey in this army uniform. So they arrested me, and put me in a hospital. They put me in four-point restraints, shot me up with thorazine. They said they were saving me from myself. Yeah, some saving! They made me walk like a zombie. I was no zombie before that damn drug. I was in Bend, Oregon when I broke my neck. No bend—a break. Maybe that's because I'm so stiff-necked, so stubborn. The doctors put me in this halo; they thought they would make me into some kinda angel. This thing, this halo, they called a hela vest. They put me in it, because I crashed my car, the one Mom bought me. You see, I had this accident. Some fucking voice spoke to me, "Go crash that tree! You don't believe in a tree of life. Go do it." All those people screaming out for family. Please, God, give me a hand. I've probably been reading too many papers like the National Enquirer and watching too much Fox news. All they do with those trees anyway is make paper for more stupid books. They invented a new word; they use recycled paper... Bull shit!!! Why don't they just let the trees be?

I'm lucky. I guess I am. I don't have leprosy, I'm not paralyzed from the waist down; my prick still works, but I think I have AIDS. I'm good looking except for the tire, my love handles, round my middle cause of the damn drugs. I get along real well with just about everybody. I'm not real courageous. I mean, this is crazy. I'm the modern Hamlet suffering from PTSD. That's post-traumatic-stress disorder. I mean now we have so many more diseases that try to answer the question: To be or not to be! They say I'm being destructive, but look at what they do! I mean the people who wanna speak out can't. They shut you up one way or another.

That g-damn ball: medulla, cerebellum, synapses, frontal lope, cerebrum, that they've been trying to figure out since god created adam and eve. BI-POLAR MANIC-DEPRESSIVE. I call it ECSTATIC/DESPAIR EXISTENTIALISM. They could have called it a tumor since life is so malignant. It would have been easier. They'd cut it out, give me chemo, radiate the hell out of me; I'd, at least, get some sympathy. Big boys don't cry; they smash up cars, walls, women, whatever stands in their way. Nobody understands all the voices crying out. I'm a battered and battering ram, sacrificed. If they'd listened to God and stayed in the damn garden rather than running around looking for trouble, everything woulda been all right. I mean God knew what he was doing. They had everything they needed there in Paradise, but they thought they could do it better. Yeah, some fucking better.

I didn't realize there'd be some other kinda pain to take its place. I crashed cars like bending Venetian blinds. You know, the way they pop back when you let go. I mean, I guess I thought I was Evil Knievel. The first crash was my friend's fault. I was fifteen; me and some friends stole a car... not actually stole it... it was waiting there for us. No license plates, just sitting in some guy's driveway. So I became the driver, and when challenged, I did the only thing a boy of my age could do in this fucked up society of war-mongering stupid challenges. I drove it over one of those mini-cliffs behind my house. I came outta that one clean. I'm a cat with nine lives. Then there was the motorcycle. I took my Dad's bike and went for a joy ride. Some joy ride! I came out with an arm that ran blood for hours and had a scab the size of Texas. That's how Mom found out. I couldn't hide the scab. She discovered it when she came to this Middle-eastern restaurant where I worked washing dishes so I could help her out. She was pissed. I was more pissed. I went to work the next day because I'd said I'd be there.

People tell me I'm lucky. I don't feel lucky. Lucky would have been getting out of here, to those pearly gates where one didn't have to make choices. But then Dad and Mom tell me that I have a lot to give and a lot to get, and that there's nothing after you leave this life. I don't know, and I don't think they do either.

Mom really doesn't believe I'm what the doctors say I am. She hasn't told me that, but I think she thinks that. You see, both my parents are crazy anyway, that's the way I see it. And I've got to figure out my own life. There's not much else for me to do while I sit in this place. When I talk to Mom about this God thing and staying in the garden and that everything was there and that God, he knew what he was doing, Ma says, are you sure it's a he; maybe it's a she or an it or a dust particle.

The one good thing about this hospital is that I get to tell the shrink my dreams. She really likes um! So why doesn't she release me? That is the question—slings and arrows, outrageous fortune—well, anyway, let me tell you my dreams. See what you think. Shall I be released or not? Well, anyway, here they are; I even gave them titles. I feel like this kindergarten kid showing and telling. Well, anyway, here are the titles; I don't know which one to tell first. The Arena Dream is probably the best, but then again, The Beaver Dream ain't so bad. The Bulldozing Dream and The Broken Bridge Rainbow Dream really confuse me.

Well, here goes: I'm this school bus driver. I've got all these kids I'm in charge of and we're going on a picnic. We get out of the school bus at some sort of park. I start running around trying to find seating and food for them all. Out of the corner of my eye I see this beaver who's encircled in white light. He's lying on his back. I notice him and go about my business trying to get enough food and space for the children. All of a sudden, I see this woman sitting with a beaver in her lap. He's brown and very happy. I look back at the white beaver who, all of a sudden turns over, and turns yellow then brown and runs down the road; his eyes are full of fear; he looks at me and runs. So what do you think? Am I afraid of sex? That's what my shrink said when I told her my dream. I don't think she really knows what I'm dreaming about. I'm not afraid of sex. I am afraid of bringing another child into this crummy world where everybody's fighting over land and needing to be more powerful than the next person. I mean, to me, that dream is about getting rid of fear and living in peace; where there's food and space enough for all, and I mean the animals too. For crying out loud! Why doesn't anybody learn from history? So, what do you think? Am I crazy? I guess so cause all I see on TV is people fighting with one another and accusing one another, and telling lies and stories. Maybe I just want my story told. Maybe I'm as bad as the next guy. So, if that's so, what am I doing here anyway?

They think it's an obsession and that I should start taking care of myself and stop worrying about the world. They got these crazy Z's painted on the walls of this hospital. What are they trying to do to us nuts?

How did I wind up here? This place drives me crazy. There's one girl here who mumbles and cries all the time. Nobody can understand her. I don't give a shit about her. I used to be compassionate! Look where it got me! I'm not gonna tell you how old I am. It doesn't matter. What I feel like matters. You see, this screamer is inside me. He's about nine years old, and all he wants to do is stop everyone from hurting him. But he can't. He doesn't know how. He's afraid to let him scream; he may scream something I don't want to hear. The only problem is that there are too many I's.

Mom was on cortisone right after she conceived me. She has this asthma thing, you see, and when she found out she was pregnant, she got terrible asthma. Maybe it's the cortisone that's made me crazy. There's something else I can blame on her. But I don't want to blame her.

There's a black and white photograph I have of my family before my sister was born. I was about two when my parents' friend, Irwin, took it. Three bodies tumbling in the grass, my mother had on this long dress; my father wore Levis and a work shirt with lots of pockets. I wore a diaper, and a plastic, rubber nipple bottle hung from my lips. I think I hung on for dear life. I don't think I ever let go of the rubber nipple. But that's okay, 'cause we all need something to hang on to. Anyway, whenever I look at that picture, I get real sad and also happy if that makes any sense. It's about memory and what it does to the heart and body.

I just want to be in the goddamn world again. I want to be on the slopes, skiing my ass off. You either know what you want to do or forget it! There we go again- rocking and rolling with the voices. You know, you can't trust other people to talk about you; so, it's better if you talk about yourself.

All I want, goddammit, is for people to get along; is for the animals to be free, the land to be green, the air to be clean, one nation, no governments, no war. I guess that's why I'm here, listening to the jangling keys, looking at the vomit green walls.

Microfiction and Prose Poems

Stars

Roberta Allen

In the White Desert where our inventive Egyptian guide spoke about a deadly snake that could leap thirty feet in the air, where the novice leader from California told us to sleep anywhere we wanted, where I, the only one in the group without a partner, was left to fend for myself but, like the others, who were soon out of sight, was also without a tent, I was unexpectedly blessed. At dusk, a rarely-seen jackal, a nocturnal creature as delicate and transparent as a glass figurine, suddenly appeared like a vision and, before it vanished, suckled the string of my sleeping bag cover. While I was handling the still moist string, the fat British magistrate, who had been on my case since the beginning of the trip, came running to inform me that the jackal was probably rabid, which meant that I, too, would probably get the disease. Her prediction, however, failed to spoil my night alone with the stars, which either lowered themselves or lifted me up. While the stars and I stared at one another, I was safe from the imaginary leaping snake and the real horned viper, from scorpions, beetles, and larger creatures that left tracks in the sand next morning around my head, and neither heard the screeching sounds nor saw the flashing lights of 4-wheel-drive emergency vehicles and whirring helicopters that arrived in the night to transport the violently retching members of the group, who had eaten the same stew I had eaten, prepared by the Bedouins, even before I knew I was protected by the stars.

Anneka

Roberta Allen

If I change her name to Anneka, will she, a drunk over fifty (to be kind), who lives (if still alive) three thousand miles away with severe osteoporosis, ever discover that I wrote about the morning several years ago when I, a naive guest, opened the door on the third floor in her canal house and found her in bed in her sleeping alcove, amidst the stench of gin and sex, snoring loudly, blankets on the floor, legs spread wide, her everything in my face, the hairy arm of a boy with a name like Theo or Pieter or Jan, sprawled across her breasts, his head resting below the dentures that had slipped down in her open mouth?

String Theory

Guy Reed

An odd thing I'd noticed one day recently was the clothes line in the side yard, it runs in a loop between two pulleys held by two trees, it was vibrating. I only look at the clothesline when I'm hanging laundry or with a peripheral glance as I duck underneath. But from 30 feet away I noticed a small blur in my field of vision and thinking it was the top loop of the clothesline vibrating I wondered if my eyes played tricks. It didn't go away when I blinked so I was drawn to it. It was vibrating. I listened for some type of hum, a car, a plane, the furnace, something that could be causing this. I touched it and it stopped, but immediately the bottom line began vibrating. Then I stopped. I relaxed and focused my concentration...the wind? No, there was nothing I could hear or feel that could be the cause of this. I touched the lower line and the top one started again. I touched it once more and it stopped altogether. Nothing but the usual sound of a quiet day. This puzzled me for a while. But I continued to wonder. Then one quiet night I heard a train whistle, must be six, seven miles away, the nearest tracks, plus, another eight hundred foot drop down the lower southeastern slope of the Catskill Mountains toward the Hudson River. I went to the clothesline and it was vibrating. I couldn't hear the train other than the whistle, maybe a very distant low rumble through six miles of air, past the pulleys, the trees, the roots, the soil, the bedrock on down slopes and ledges covered in woods and littered with streams, fields, homes, and pastures, past schools, businesses, neighborhoods, bridges, and the NY State Thruway. Past all of that rumbles a locomotive steel on steel, waves ripple from its motion on track.

Love, Death, Etc.

Howard Good

1

My mother scoops snow off the fire escape into the kitchen pot. Her hands dart like birds. I'm four, maybe five. It's snowing for the first time, but I'm sick with something and can't go out. She carries the snow to the bathtub where she bathes my brother and me, scrubbing us in a kind of rage until our skin is as rosy as the bottoms of angels. After she dumps the snow from the pot, I kneel outside the tub and play with it, not knowing what I'll remember one day or that no one escapes the fire.

2

Someone asks, "Have you written anything yet about your mother's death?" No. . . no, I haven't. There aren't any angels to consult, and that if there were, they'd hurl themselves like despondent drunks onto the gleaming knives and spears of the spires below. Instead, only birds scatter at the approach of dark, and I try not to see too much, the forgeries and desecrations, or the black snow collecting on the floor of my heart.

3

Then it's spring, a year since the failed operation, the road into town smeared with blood and entrails, and a quorum of crows crowding around what's left, hungry, contentious, but to me, simply driving past, it looks different, like a blob of God's spit.

4

Where we sleep, you know, it isn't necessarily where we wake up, it all depends on what we dream, my dead mother, for example, crisscrossed by the fence, fingers hooked through the diamond-shaped links.

Imagine

R.E. Rigolino

More than the seeing was the smelling. Sharp. Bitter. Metallic. Yet, a trace of the earth remained.

It was early, so the crowds had not gathered. Maybe twenty. Perhaps thirty people circled quietly, politely taking turns on the dumpster or the random chair someone had brought. The fence was high, and they talked in small whispers, sometimes softly laughing with embarrassment when they weren't agile, but always solemn at the ascent.

When it was my turn, I climbed, but it was the smell that absorbed my attention. It wrapped around me, slowly constricting my throat so that I couldn't swallow. My throat burned. I quickly jumped down.

"Are you a resident?" Her unexpected smile was lovely. Sweet. She was very young. Maybe twenty. She wore an official vest and a baseball cap stamped with the name of a relief agency.

I shook my head, wheezing.

A frown shadowed her lips, but then trailed off. There was a flicker. "Here," she smiled again and thrust out a magic marker. "Here. You can leave a message." She pointed to the multicolored layers of paper that were stapled, tacked, and pounded into a plywood fence. Words were everywhere: some desperately scribbled, others carefully chosen, decorated with a flourish of swirls, hearts, flowers.

REST IN PEACE America will <u>never</u> forget! Our ♥ R With U ALL!!!! The sleeping giant is awake/You had better quake! Imagine all the people living life in piece, You may say that I'm a dreamer But I'm not the only one................

She pointed to some as examples. "You know, you could leave a message. A note. A prayer."

I hesitated. She expertly tucked a loop of curly brown hair back up under her baseball cap. I could sense she was beginning to tire of me. She looked slightly beyond my left shoulder. Only for a moment though.

"Just a short sentence or two. Something to leave behind for other people to read."

Accepting finally, I took up the marker and moved in the direction she was now pointing to. A small space on an already crowded banner. I stared at the six by three inch space, now empty, waiting to be filled.

The smell. The smell was all I could think of. How could someone read the smell? I searched for a sentence. Maybe two. I grasped for words, but they kept slipping away, like rabbits into the undergrowth at the forest's edge.

Mute, I handed the marker back and began the long walk north.

The God of Falling Objects

Christine Boyka Kluge

Perhaps you've felt her blue stare, cold as sea glass. She never shuts her all-seeing eyes. She silently watches your keys tumble from your pocket, jingling their unheard brass alarm. When your wedding ring slides from your finger like a greased halo, she doesn't even flinch. Come October, leaves spiral past her indifferent face. She lets them go, never blinking, never beckoning them back to your maple's empty branches.

She watches impassively as babies, dizzy with first steps, teeter at the tops of stairs, as flowerpots twitch on window ledges. She observes the inevitable trajectories of flawed angels and jets, numb to the fiery amber and emerald beauty of both meteorites and bombs. Falling tears and eggs, skyscrapers and mountains—they're all the same, plummeting as insignificantly as scrapings from burnt toast. It's useless to try to catch the crumbs of the crumbling universe. It would be absurd to hold out her arms.

Doesn't anyone else notice? The sky is opening its mouth. She can see into its black throat, that shining tunnel of star dust and salt. Apparently only she hears the faint, terrible sound of heaven swallowing its own milky tongue.

The Woman With The Video Camera

Bruce Weber

she videotaped the way rain fell in hard diagonals/the white
noise emanating from the grayness of the tv screen/how the
atmosphere affected personality disorders/how the weather
shaped the destinies of muslims/the bouncing of children on
beds while the babysitter was sleeping/the arrangement of
mirrors of tables of lamps of pictures on walls/how light
coated ever face/how hair grows on a head/she videotaped
the textures of surrender/the cool breath of a stranger on a
neck/the hand's passage up a thigh/the soft pressing of fingers
on a groin/she aimed her camera at the runners jogging/the
dinner parties foiled by a burnt chicken/the drunken antics
of an uncle puffing cigar smoke/the geometry of windows
maintaining their rigid attitude against the dirt/she turned
the camera on the reunion of mothers and daughters/the
warm creasing embrace/the kisses upon cheekbones/the
visitations of grandchildren on xmas/the streamers extending
out of mouths on new year/the traffic inside whore houses/
the movement of men entering rooms removing hats removing
gloves removing scarfs removing topcoats removing pants
removing undergarments/she videotaped every nuance of color/
every pore marking survival/every grip on the banister/every
foot rising up/every shoe being tied/her eyes absorbing the
protocol of nightlight saying come undress me with your camera
penetrate every dominion

Poetry: Hudson Valley Views

Swimming In The Hay Barn

Barbara Adams

Yesterday
I rode my bike south
along the muddy Wallkill River
winding perversely north.

My legs pumped hard
as the corn ripened into stiff shafts
smelling of love's breath.

Clouds melted like icebergs
in the ocean of sweet
Canadian air
mixing with valley humidity.

Dappled with shadows
I drove through fields of corn-
stubble and blue asters
brighter than stars.

Four miles from town
Ellie's barn loomed
like a cool cave in the sun.
Ellie and I swung

Barbara Adams

Through a cloud of boys
on a thick rope, one by one,
drifting down on a sunbeam,
whirling like motes of dust.

We landed on the pillow
of hay below
still children—and rose
Grown up.

The Laws of What Happens
(The Lefevre farmhouse, Route 32 North)

Jacqueline Renée Ahl

We are skeletons buttoning sweaters against poverty's law:
a lowered thermostat
gap-tooth windows
the wind's low wolf whistle.
Gone are the backyard pears freckled by the beaks
of curious birds
the stew and sympathy of your mother's Monday leftovers.
Here are the baby mice bashed after a botched trap
in "us-or-them" agony
—without bread there is death—
your lowered head mourning the hammer's fall.
Here is the compost of bills. The monolith of dishes.
Here are the tapered fingers of candles
while metered filaments sleep.
Outside, tires on wet pavement tear like hospital gowns—
the insistent ambulance whine of "now"
anonymous speeding Suburbans that mow cats to cadavers,
orange leaves spiraling after.
The faster all else moves, the slower our motions become:
conserve heat, money, love.
An hour of stirring while steam spirals up to finger the drapes,
twelve nights to finish a novel,
spine cracking in stretches between.

Jacqueline Renée Ahl

The heaters stir and knock, wavering at 64.
Slowly the water seizes,
hardens in a silver ribbon along the road
ages the grass, a cryogenic death for prehistoric crickets,
green spears, spiders.
The laws of what happens.
But some nights we seem able to break them:
gravity, possibility, the stamina of hope.
Commodities exchange in the tracer lights of traffic—
ferried gurneys
loaded carts and barreling delivery vans.
The more insistent hell's breath, the more candles we prop
on tables,
in windows, burning ovals into dusk.
They illuminate confusion, warm knuckles,
strobe the axe-hewn beams
laughing us out of sweaters and into sheets,
or the soft profusion of socks and towels
on the closet floor, rows of shirt sleeves tickling our heads.
Lightyears of eyelashes and arms.
Suddenly we are forgetting
the brown pear mash sinking into the soil
the last heel of bread curling in a bag
the assault against armies of rodents and air,
chinks stuffed with steel wool and rags
the suckerpunch of minimum wages
and middle class firing squads.
Suddenly mouth to mouth is saving us,
an army of stars glimmering bodies with applause.
Suddenly the world costs nothing.
The future is water pinging hard on a tin roof,

our dabbled adjectives and lobbed lines,
a sign above the bed-post urging "*forgive.*"
Suddenly we do.

The Carrion Eaters

David Appelbaum

All day orange blades flash
in cold weak light.

It is too clear for death.

Instead they plume and circle
the stanchions on the Ed building
feigning to stray

Gaunt crows who otherwise run
the rutted tarmac roof
snap below the flag

The others are various and thick
conquerors east
from mountain rooks, now
raiders of local trash heaps.

Among microwave antennas
ten stories up, they brood
an apocalypse forsaken

vast silent hunchbacks
glare at a protectorate

no hussar would dare brave.

Rite of Passage

David Appelbaum

hitch down from Albany on secondary
roads in April early
     sun enough to red
     the face of noon

     Connecticut line
     thin with cars
     and winter potholes

the force of a clenched fist
keeps driving along, fear
the wrong message sent

but to more than one
they stop for a son,
theirs, on the same highway strand
thumb awkward out
for the next ride home

and when the Chevy door opens finally,
whose boyhood then looks in?

Tree Watching

Brenda Connor-Bey

On the Taconic

Why do I hold my breath every time
I see a stand of trees? A sigh of awe escapes
as my car passes them. Trees remind me
of women, sisters dancing in a sacred circle
Stonehenge revisited
mountain mists and fog snake along
upheld arms, reaching for sky

It's not any special season when
this ache of awe and wonder descends
when the willow weeps its first hint of pale green
sketching its way into veins
in temperatures frigid enough
for glove wearing

In winter their skeletal darkness lay
open to fierce winds that
crack open their life's blood

BRENDA CONNOR-BEY

The Bronx River Parkway

I love the shape of these dancers
just above the rise of north and south
A bevy of wild-hipped sisters
here, grey and silent
waiting for their Mother's call
to sleep naked and twisted
ignored except for birds, squirrels
and, I believe, my eyes

Spring Walks, Mountain Views

James Finn Cotter

I   Climbing Thomas Cole

Some day in late May,
Air clean as cucumbers,
Follow the scraped-to-silver
Red trail markers
To Thomas Cole Mountain
In the Northern escarpment
Of the Catskill range.

Climbing Thomas Cole
Forget your knapsack,
Guidebook, and canteen.
Take a sandwich and apple
And drink the brook water
Below the caudal ledge
Before reaching the first ridge.

Climbing Thomas Cole
You find the path peopled
With awakening wildlife:
Fiddleheads in snow swatches,
Bluets, violets, and wood sorrel,

JAMES FINN COTTER

Purple trillium and gentian,
Liverwort and lily-of-the-valley.

Climbing Thomas Cole
You walk on flagged shale,
Pink-veined quartz in sandstone,
And moss-bulging boulders,
On tree bark and split limbs,
Leaf litter, mold, and fronds,
Fir needles in the black loam.

Climbing Thomas Cole
You pass hardwood forest
And tenantless pastureland,
Snow spurs in beech shadow,
And bracket fungus on bur oak,
Lightning stroke of paper birch
In a green shower of balsam.

Climbing Thomas Cole
You hear song sparrow and thrush,
The blackbird's sentry call,
And woodpecker's needlework.
Watch for the wary red fox,
The chipmunk and porcupine
And white-plume-tailed deer.

Climbing Thomas Cole
You hike from the trailhead
Up the red-clay embankment
Packed down hard by the boot soles
Of the hikers before you,

Through woods of hemlock and pine
To the gray-shiny rock face.

Climbing Thomas Cole
You look out from the summit
On a horseshoe of highlands
From Elm Ridge to Acra Point,
North and South Mountains,
From High Peak to West Kill,
Pitched parabolas of hills.

Climbing Thomas Cole
You trace the Devil's Path
On Indian Head, Twin, Sugarloaf,
From his Kitchen to Tombstone,
And in Stony Clove Notch
Between Plateau and Hunter
See Slide lifted in sunlight.

Climbing Thomas Cole
One day in late May,
Sky clear as Lake Colgate,
Watch the shifts in Mink Hollow
As clouds brindle the woodland.
Then circle back down to Maplecrest
By way of Black Dome and Blackhead.

JAMES FINN COTTER

II Ashokan

From the southwestern ledge of Overlook Mountain
I gaze down with open view of the Ashokan Reservoir
Gleaming at noon in the far level valley
Like a prospect discovered on another planet

Or like a scaly-blue apocalyptic dragon
Become the sparkling liquid it has spewed:
Between Panther Mountain and High Point as background,
Dappled with clouds, the reservoir lolls in the sun.

River and brook, lake and pool, in confluence
Join here for weir, waterfall, and aqueduct
To run from Kingston to Manhattan the diamond element
That millions drink daily out of chromium faucets.

Ashokan, seen from Wittenberg and Cornell Mountains
With Overlook drifting opposite, east-northeast,
Man-shaped crystal, cauldron, mirror, mouth,
Your surface brimming like buckets out of wells,

The primal miracle is water let down from the sky,
For, as old myths say, gods portioned out the two:
Opening a tent to hold the upper water up,
They stored the lower sky in bowls at their feet.

III Artist's Rock

Walking from North Lake to North Mountain
From the site of the Catskill Mountain House,
Be sure to stop and visit Artist's Rock
To see the Hudson Valley smooth as canvas,
The river splashed on like a streak of paint.

On this sheer cliff a century ago
Men in black waistcoats and white collars
Strolled arm in arm with bustled ladies
In blue silk blouses and trailing skirts,
As straight as easels set before the scene.

Today the campers crowd between the pines,
Their maroon station wagons and beige trailers
Parked in designated lots along the shore.
Cooking out of doors by woods and lake,
They spend the night in sleeping bags and tents.

If you take the blue-blazed pathway over
The crest of North Mountain to Stoppel Point,
Follow the red trail markers down the slope
Where wind dabs the silver-green beech leaves
And brushes of light touch the lichen and weeds.

JAMES FINN COTTER

IV The Fire Tower

1

When at last I hiked up Tremper Mountain,
I found the lookout tower standing abandonded,
The ground stage without its stairway steps,

The first deck opened and without a floor.
I saw the scaffolding and cabin vandalized,
Its high windows all shot out by hunters.

I squatted at the base and contemplated
The wreckage of my stranded, would-be ark:
The hard climb up had been for nothing.

2

Then on the glass-strewn, scrubby glacial knob
I discovered a discarded picnic table
Tossed on its side, the seats in splinters,

Like an old rowboat scuttled on dry land.
Hauling it against the struts and railing
And using the split planks as foothold rungs,

I shimmied up the floorless platform,
At one point hanging tautly horizontal,
A hand and ankle fastening me in space.

Like ladder supported wrong end over,
The suspended stairs led down to nowhere
But kept a pendulous grip on leading up.

I walked the tightrope rod that held them
And slowly mounted step by swaying step,
With both hands reaching to the boards above.

I drew my two knees up onto the floor,
Rolled over and, sprawled out on the deck,
Lay gasping like a fish flat on my back.

My heart pounded in my rib cage, drowning.
I closed my eyes and, breathing out the air,
Sank into the sunlight's sea of flame.

A net of shimmering sweat broke from my face.
I blinked up at the tower, tier on tier,
Its raked masts and rigging set for sail.

I rose and, steadied by the iron handrail,
Scaled the seven steep-ascending stories;
Then cautiously I clambered to the top.

I crept out from the open-wide trap door
And, mounted upward on the plank-lined floor,
Gazed down, aloft, at the surrounding scene.

3

Standing the stringed center of a bow
That arches northeastward from Red Hill
To Balsam Mountain and Windham High Peak,

I felt the arrow of my mind spring free
And strike the bull's eye of a further Self.
From pinnacles of evergreen and clouds

JAMES FINN COTTER

Sailing resplendent in the sea-blue valley
To the lone crow's nest relay-station tower,
The hills around me beamed the diamond sun.

Through shattered windows agape to the sky
The cabin filled with wave on wave of light,
And I knew: Lord, it is good that I am here

To look out on the waters of these skies
And see reflected mountains, trees, and fields:
My heart is fire and one within your target.

You are the rainbow, ladder, mast, and star,
Way of the woods and brook and wind and daybreak
And blossoms without end.

4

Step by step lightly down the seven stages
I eased back down the way I had climbed up,
Slipped to the last two airy decks, the stairs

Hanging weightless and wobbly in empty space,
And leapt to the glittering, grassy ground below,
And—lest the strongman at midnight walk

Away with it, as Chuang Tsu has warned—
Hiding the universe within the universe,
I stored the table in the underbrush.

Farewell To Summer

Lynne Digby

Loostrife's rusted and ragweed heavy with bloom.
Soft shadows slant, and restless birds fly by.
September's sun, a hazy orange sphere, hangs
where ghostly hills lie shrouded in layered bands of fog.
Soft mist-ribbons rise from summer's sun-warmed waters.
And morning dew drops hang on untouchable
cobweb loops strung in sunlit spaces.
A galaxy of water diamonds
sparkling on summer's dress of blazing color.
Michaelmas daisies, regally purple,
midst clouds of yellow, lavender and white.

Lovely summer, how brilliantly she paints,
with wild and magnificent abandon.
Caring not a whit that Fall,
with one flash of his frosty fingers
will wipe the glorious colors from her palette.

The days pull close, their time cut short.
A death chill shivers the damp evening air.
Sweet summer whispers of farewells, and moving southward.
Would that I could traipse behind her dancing heels.
I mourn her leaving. She will return I know,
but never, no, not ever soon enough for me.

Designs

Dennis Doherty

I don't know what the word meant to her,
as she plucked wild flowers and found
that fawn like a diamond of compressed story
picked over by thieving bugs and mice,
its bright bones whiting in the sun.

"I don't like it," she said, when I
stooped to stuff my pockets with pieces.
"Don't." "Just the jaws and skull then,
to decorate the garden. Show Mom."
She stamped her feet, looked to the wood.
"I don't like designs," she whined. "I'm scared."

The pit was a muddy frog bath webbed
above by birch and oak and the birds who
sing there, the wood hemmed by vermicular
lines of homes and roads whose roars
influenced the leaves. The fawn lay
like a neatly mounted puzzle, its sloughed
pelt sewn into ground by slaving insects,
its teeth feeding weeds.

"The designs," she said, "they scare me."
"You mean the bugs crawling on the fur?"
She stepped back, and I caught her at the edge.
"Does my brother look like that?" I wondered
at the gnarled arc of vertebrae and ribs bowed
like boat slats. "He's ashes," I said, "in
a box at home." She hugged her loosestrife.
"Let's go back to Momma. Maybe you can bring his jaws."

Feet

Dennis Doherty

—We found it right in our yard! A dead muskrat!
*—Yeah, but dead birds are almost natural 'cause they fall out of
   their nests.*
                    —overheard schoolboys

Birds do fall from nests like fruit.
A storm cloud dislodges drops
and raps the first ripe berry. Damned
slugs gnaw everywhere at red and green;
mucus rises on moisture, from earthworm
castings to the columbine stars.
The trees, the ozone, the mole-run ground
tremble with colliding, migrant flight.

Their mystery's in the muskrat,
having left its lodge and flopped
on foreign soil beneath the eggs
of robins at this boy's home
where small shoes have known the grass away,
his own dirt an unsifted pan
of sneaker-kneaded past,
a history of bug and leaf debris.
If we could only teach boy's feet to see.

Summer Stage in Winter

Allen C. Fischer

Shuttered in silence, now and then
the great shed echoes a custodian's scuff
as he makes the rounds, muttering the wind's lisp.
The festival grounds have returned to gray,
trees to bone, lawns a dull thatch. Then, poco
a poco, in coda to all the symphonies of summer,
the heavy clouds begin their notion of music,
not with voice or hands but single flakes, white
notes so soft they're not heard at all.
Here, there, they drift down, spare at first,
making the very thought of pianissimo seem
distant, and crescendo out of the question.
Like grace notes, they come as if
to test the terrain, fathom the possibility.

Overhead, the clouds rehearse
the lungs of what aired months before.
As the weather quickens, ideas begin
to swarm, their downfall forming and
reforming into swirls, loose bodies,
ghostly shapes, the snow silencing everything
so the air can compose.

ALLEN C. FISCHER

And there, in a theater of mime,
out of the cosmic rhythm that beats time, comes
the withered spirit of Vivaldi playing "Winter,"
comes a scowl of Beethoven's "Grosse Fugue,"
comes Shostakovich's blizzard of notes
and white noise of such hallucination
the matter of music harks back to single voices:
to coyote, raccoon, hawk when they began
on snow's blank page, waiting winter's down-beat.

November Kill

Mala Hoffman

Even at a distance
you could tell
that the mound
behind the above-ground pool
had once been alive.
The way the surface
yielded slightly
as the young boy
stood aloft in his boots
as though seeing
the New World
for the first time.
He grabbed onto antlers
tugging the mass
closer to his cocker spaniel
dipping his fingers
into the liquid pot of the entry point
and sniffing them.

Woodstock Mornings

C.J. Krieger

The reservoir sparkled
While dancing with the sun
As they walked hand in hand
Along the well worn path
That circled the waters edge

No sounds of city traffic
Or early mornings movement
Could be heard anywhere about
Only two voices constantly repeating
Declarations of affection

Lost within each others eyes
Embracing each time they stopped
With buns and coffee
From the early breakfast
Completing the Catskill dawn

My Hermit

Robert Leaver

I am quite wealthy
Mansion on the Hudson
Hundreds of acres
River frontage and forest
Fields and burbling brooks
I pay a man to live alone
In the woods
His hair is long and matted
Nails are never to be cut
He bathes in the summer
And wears a burlap tunic
I visit him and he's supposed to tell me
What it's like to be so alone
Reflecting on solitude
The wisdom of nature
He gets paid every seven years
I provide food and a bible
He stopped speaking last winter
I may have to let him go.

Carpentry & Gardening

Phillip Levine

I have broken hearts through the careless use of lilac and hammer

Pounded salt like nails into the thinnest wounds and split the wood

I have twisted the root back upon itself to knot and choke

Left the splinters of fine things in my fingers to pus and swell
Breathed the dust of the dowel cut and rabbet run

I have let the saw tooth rust in the rain

Buried flower beds in yards of mud and for many seasons seen only the crack of grass between the rock

I have built crooked stairs that climb to empty places
hung doors where windows go
and placed clear glass in entry paths

I have picked the peach hard like nut

I have cut the stem before the bloom and scent

PHILLIP LEVINE

I have ripped the headboard ragged

Still,
I have both hands and all my fingers
and I can still feel the raised grain of moistened wood
and smell the wild queen's lace
and see the tulip's glow

And now,
I have made this plain and simple
Flower box of clean straight edge
Rich in soil and well drained with stone
This plot is ready for seed, sun and water

Rt. 44/55 at night

Nadine Lewis

beyond the road there is a blanket of stars
waving in the air like a sheet being reset on the bed in morning
dangerously swerving close to the guardrail
I remember the scenic route is really a pleasure
    best served in light
now, night driving—hair pins turns, an uneasy adornment
    to the road
makes my hair stand on end
and the town lights make it hard to tell where the sky stops
and the earth begins

Autumn Vintage

Robert Milby

The age of the vine...
Sun shifts in late Summer

And the vintner spills dark wine
On the dusty floor of a pungent barn.

Ripe apples, some variegated, load gnarled trees
Like Yule ornaments on resplendent boughs.

Breezes cough myriad tapestries of bold, floral color;
Each hardwood emblazoned by an original painter.

This candor of October wind—fallen acorns and chestnuts—
New pigment on mossy forest lawns.

Full-figured pumpkins and their kindred, glow fire hue,
    where only months before,
Blossoms and young vines hosted honeybee and butterfly
    Bacchanals.

Strange October clouds spend afternoons licking morning frost
From cold skin of the orange goddess,

ROBERT MILBY

Leaves soaked in Tannic acid tea;
Chilled bog placenta from Summer pond gestations.

A young woman walks down the hill, admiring the shifting
    countenance of the field
As North wind tickles nipples to jut beneath a red wool sweater.

She admonishes the bold wind, like a teasing lover. Her hair
    is burnt mustard.
Maple leaves bluster like saffron tinged rags tossed into the sky.

The Bridge has no cars to ruin it;
Wallkill's banks brew fog for Maple branches.

The lake in the sky calls to her.
She owns this ephemeral autumn vintage, this fugitive of harvest.

Sister Scarecrows
– *Cottekill Fire House Community Garden*

Will Nixon

Drunk? Or simply exhausted? The scarecrow slumps
in a castoff chair. Her faceless nylon stocking
stuffed with newspapers for a head
flops backwards to stare at the flawless sky
that hasn't rained since July. Her work gloves
magic-marked "BOSS" across the knuckles
lay empty on her lap. With one ankle
skinny as a broomstick & the other
no ankle at all, she sits like a starveling
before her crop of stunted vines.

But her sister, dressed in similar green sweats
that forgive her sagging breasts & spreading hips,
sits upright & alert, her straw hat tipped
outrageously sideways with bohemian flare.
Her name tag says "Sunshine." Her work gloves
cradle a dirt-cheeked doll with blue eyes & golden hair.
She's slipped off her leather pumps
& snuggled her broomsticks in raspberry brambles,
now ripening with fruit despite the drought.
Watering my peppers, I swear she asks for a cigarette.

WILL NIXON

Then she whispers that her bitter sister
has become a desert mystic
convinced the seed she planted will be the burning bush.
She, herself, would settle for a good mint julep
& a man who still believes in wearing teeth.

The Life of the Stag
– *Catskills*

Will Nixon

You nibbled sharply on my lips, testing:
You just want a girlfriend to help you carry logs.
I held you bony & damp in my lap,
studied the cheek mole you said children loved to touch.
And go to the movies with, I said.
Your black Manhattan jeans lay dropped
on the fire rug by my rubber-soled Wolverines.
Smoke leaked from my wood stove like a cigarette.

In the morning we snowshoed Cross Mountain.
I showed you beech trees graffitied by bear claws
the size of our hands & told you my story:
after the Hoboken divorce, I chose these mountains,
hung a Cherokee mask by my door,
filled my pencil holder with wild turkey feathers,
wrote my first ode to porcupines.

Then I found my Inner Wendigo
named after the Indian spirit in a low-budget movie
shot one winter by our reservoir.
Half-deer loaded with antlers like bone chandeliers,
half-human in buckskin leggings,

this creature hurdled like an Olympian
through the midnight forest while strobe lights
flashed beech trees, fierce as totem poles.
And what was the Wendigo chasing? you asked.
The same old story, I said, *revenge.*
We kissed, turning me back into a man.

Heron

Jo Pitkin

Heron shadowed my house today,
   slicing the stillness of my now-life,
      wing of gray feather. . . .

Bird of my marshes, my reedy bogs.
   River dweller, fisher, rooter and raider
      of swamp and shore.

Heron stalked my swirling river today,
   listening for surface burble or splash,
      prey, predator, prey.

Bird of salt and eddy, wound of the beloved,
   pond darter, still tracker, dancer in shallows
      on weed and water.

In the white tundra of my losses,
   no herons nest in blackgold stalks
      over a cache of eggs,

no herons spear the repetitious pattern
   of wave wave wave or scatter powder down
      like milk-ripe fieldweed.

Jo Pitkin

Only the wind whispers today
   as I lie flat on gravel waiting for heron
      to hover over me

searching for water, for tide, for streamside,
   its long neck looping in an S to spell
      in a cloudless, chilly sky

the letter for sorrow, seed, savior,
   the iconographic hook, the sound of the sea,
      suitor, son, saint, sire.

Stone House
from a 1934 Walker Evans' photograph of the Crane home, Somers, New York

Jo Pitkin

In the foreground, a few silvered strips of fence. The
yard's topiary made from light. I see a gravel path like
a brush of yellow dust. Monument. In the center,
shadows move on granite like dark moss, and dark ivy
mosses stone. An iron fence of spikes gates the wild.
Pastoral brush. Twin giant pines shine tinseled by
hanging heavy cones. As November sun spills
silvered coins over dark moss shadows and stark cones
of pillars, a tinsel stain darkens light granite. Twin
chimneys fence off the background. Now the focus is
the iron-stained door, from which, all at once, a man
in a gravel-colored suit, perhaps smoking the hollow
cone of a cigar or cradling a rolled paper, may appear.
The hidden conversation between roof top, tree
branch, sky.

The Dogs and I Walked Our Woods,

Gretchen Primack

and there was a dog, precisely the colors of autumn,
asleep between two trunks by the trail.
But it was a coyote, paws pink
with a clean-through hole in the left,
and a deep hole in the back of the neck,
dragged and placed in the low crotch
of a tree. But it was two coyotes,
the other's hole in the side of the neck,
the other with a dried pool of blood below
the nose, a dried pool below the anus,
the other dragged and placed
in the adjoining low crook, the other's body
a precise mirror of the first. The eyes were closed,
the fur smooth and precisely the colors
of autumn, a little warm to my touch though the bodies
were not. The fur was cells telling themselves
to spin to keep her warm to stand
and hunt and keep. It was a red
autumn leaf on the forest floor, but
it was a blooded brown leaf, and another, because
they dragged the bodies to create a monument

to domination, to the enormous human.
And if I bore a child who suffered to see this,
or if I bore a child who gladdened to see this, or if
I bore a child who kept walking, I could not bear
to live, or to feed that child, so I will not bear one.

Helping My Parents' Friends Get in Hay

Matthew J. Spireng

All I was to do was ride the haywagon
and stamp down the loose hay as Frieda
or Otto tossed it up with a pitchfork.

The mound grew and I rose higher and
I don't remember at all now nearly
fifty years later how I even got down,

though I must have gotten down, and
I don't remember if it was Frieda or Otto
who pitched up the hay or drove the tractor,

or if we had water to drink in the field, or if
I helped at the barn, or if I walked home after,
or if I was paid anything at all, or if that mattered.

Brook

Matthew J. Spireng

No name now and never was one
I know of. It rises out of the ground
up in the neighbor's woods and flows down

the little gorge it's cut, baring bedrock shale
some places, dropping down over the lip
of a ten-foot falls, meandering where

it levels, never more than a foot or two wide,
and never dry, and, if the valley it's made
where the earth is soft and one side clay

is true sign, it's been flowing since long before
anyone could have put its name to paper. But then
it may have had a name, spoken only, the place

where fresh water flowed, the place where
deer would drink, their word for brook not
known now, nor their word for deer, nor for man.

Cutting the Oak

Matthew J. Spireng

There's no way to tell before cutting it
just how old it is. But you know it's huge
and it's old. You could figure its height and
diameter, measure its circumference.
You know its weight exceeds yours in the first
foot of its height. Now you want to bring it
down to your level. You study it, gauge
where you want it to fall. But what if you're
wrong? What if it says no? What if it fights
back, resists, says as your blades tear at its
heart that's the way I go, over there is
where I've planned my fall, where I grow to lie?
What then will you do but step back in awe
and listen?

Ulster Heights, New York

Christine Lilian Turczyn

As children, we looked out of our windows
when the aged reverend and his wife set out,
every evening, to row. From our perspective,
they were spirits of trees,
etiolation of grief against a negative
of sky.
The street had no lights, and we heard
their footsteps long after they passed: It was as though
everything they loved and sought to feed
hungered without name.
We imagined their lives before this summer:
A famine survived,
memories like herbs that did not grow here,
suitcases left on banks,
lost letters—fireflies rising.
No one understood,
why they pulled more fish out of that lake
than anyone.
Other seasoned fishermen imagined moonlight
carving circles on still water—scrimshaw of history against
silence,
or silence—
obverse of song's rising bread.

Christine Lilian Turczyn

Somehow, the lake yielded up its secrets
catch after catch.
But we knew it was the heart they listened for,
glittering with relentless scales,
unforgiving, fiery, and brutal,
as the war they fled,
night after night,
in sleep.
In truth,
it was love they plumbed—
nothing less than a net slipping soundlessly
over
a boat's mottled side, returning,
again and again
with forgotten life.

The Boardwalk

Nancy Williard

Who called for this trail? Not the thrush, who needs none
and whose tongue has no peep or syllable for drown.
Not the water striders, who dance on the shroud of the drowned,
which is also the sky over the trout's nest.
The boardwalk is planked like a dock, it is what I need
to enter the freshwater marsh on the hem of the bay
and speak with the herons, who think I am one of them,
standing as still as they and fishing for what I love,
the poplar shaking the light off itself like a dog,
the muffled torches of cattails, the smokebush shaky as sand
and the water lilies in bud unpacking their crowns,
their round leaves slit, like clocks with one hour lost
and water sounds the same as the word for land.

Poetry: Other Realms

Stargazing

Jay Albrecht

Star-whirled in space,
swirling astronomes corrode
light-years of blackness —yet find room, still.
Of worlds like mine, a thousand,
wide-thrown by fiery arms.
Ten living suns to each...
and a billion sheep
on far, celestial farms.

Mountain Laurel Children

Kat Alexander

The red door sweats electric in a sea of matte
A streaky garland of fingermarks to remind me,
How small a child's hand can be

Some days there is nothing but caffeine to revive me,
the absurdity of aging, its shriveled obscurity
      lessens
faced with the derisive anchor of it
how it robs us of freshness, of mischief and vivacity
My skin threatens a single peel of suicide
And I salve it back with moisturizer

Citrus safety, blusher flushed as rosacea

Other days it's the milk clotting in the bottle that binds me
The scent of cream transitioning
Reminds me
I've missed a few days. I've lost something I could have written.
The neglected workout rebels internal: my flesh softening
    from apathy
        Those days the register shorts me out of spite,
           the scary mail discarded in dense spasms so the orange
bucket teeters

Tuesdays and Thursdays the mountain laurel children pass
through the market two by two
Hooked into giant cotton moths, the safety of units
    each one a large wing flapping, dazed by cluttered summer windows,
        my ice cream chalkboard lures them toward the
        blazing light

Their endless bob and tinkle
only knows of entrances in their immensity
The graspable brink of new spaces
the prospect of a world more vivid than they've seen
devoid of matchstick carrots, curfewed cartoons,
    a room to enter warrants vocal explosion,
moist palm slaps on wood
shrieking, guzzling, irrepressible life:
    we're here, we are here – we are here

These days a room is just my confine, what keeps me in
to watch from printed windows as you pass,
Thinking:
    Keep going, just keep going

Sometimes A Buddha Poem

Jerrice Baptiste

Sometimes a Buddha poem just writes itself
With such ease
Like the sitting
....And the doing of nothing,
of nothing... unnecessary.

Such ease–
No fingers, no eyes, no lips, no tongue, no thoughts
To manipulate
that which is so simple.

Such ease
Can you imagine?

No more awkwardness of words
from a crowded mind.

Sometimes a Buddha poem
Reveals itself
With such ease
When I let go

It becomes so simple
like the sitting
...And the doing of nothing,
              of nothing... unnecessary.

Tapestry

Lucia Cherciu

"What can I give you," Mother says,
"To take back with you tomorrow when you leave?"

To my surprise Mother takes out a tapestry
She wove for her dowry as a young girl.
She got married at eighteen and before that
She had to spin her own wool after washing it in the river
She dyed the threads herself and picked the pattern.

"Let's go out on the porch in the light
So you can see the colors better," she says,
And we step outside
Holding up
The tapestry fifteen feet by five.
It smells of lavender and tobacco leaves
Carefully wrapped to keep the moths away.
Its wild flowers
Tangled in dozens of reds and greens
Soft hints of oranges,
Gentle pinks and yellows.

"It took me a whole winter to weave it," Mother says,
"Sometimes I had to unweave the threads
If the colors clashed or the warp was too loose.
We kept the loom in the main room and I stayed up
By the gas light, squinting and breathing in the smoke
Till the embers in the stove died down and my fingers got cold."
Then Mother looks up.
"Take it with you to America.
I'm sure they've never seen anything like that."

The sun dances in the soft colors of the flowers
As we spread the tapestry on the banister to air it
And keep the hungry moths away.
"Thank you, Mother, but I'm afraid.
At the customs they'd suspect I robbed the Cloisters
    or something."

"I know what you're thinking," Mother says,
"You're ashamed to hang it up on the walls. Use it as a carpet
    if you want.
I don't mind,
What else can I give you to take back?"

"Let's make a pact then," I say.
"Wait till I buy a house and then I'll take it."

Mother traces the patterns of the flowers with her hand,
Shakes off invisible specks of dust
And picks up the lint on the dark wool.
Meanwhile, I try to imagine
What the tapestry would look like on the walls

Lucia Cherciu

Of my small apartment in New York,
The wild flowers taking over,
Their warp and weft
Weaving and unweaving all night
Tugging at the loose threads.

Can the Cactus Know the Salamander

Samuel Claibourne

Can the outstretched arms of the Mantis
Know the incatching gaze of the Tarsier
Its lambent eyes reflecting mist and green

What of ocean and mountain
Can they talk of salinity and cloudburst
Rain shadow and thermocline

The mesa and the
Flat asphalt sprawl
Can they abide together
The taste and smell of
Hot summer thundershower
The cracking chafe of invading seed
And the friable winds of winter

Can the continents feel their own drift
And do they feel the Milkweed silks
That caress them with a ghost's touch
But a touch nonetheless

SAMUEL CLAIBOURNE

Do the resinous Turpentine Pines
Recognize the refinery's fumes
Or Freesia's tantric scent
In their own tang

And audacious sociable Crow
What does he think of us
Does he laugh at our differences
Or cock his head and puzzle
Over his nagging sense of kinship

These clues of consonance whisper
Informing every thing
Of every other thing

Exchanging math for sense
Schemata for intuition
Form for function
And back again

One has only to listen
Because the conversation
Is endless

Magnificent

Suzanne Cleary

In the grocery store parking lot there is
    a maroon station wagon with leopard seats,
above the front left wheel a patch of rust
    one could only call magnificent until one sees
the hood, studded with plastic tops from aerosol spray cans,
    each glued rim-down to the faded paint,
42 tops in all the known neons, black, white,
    and some colors for which there mercifully
are no names, for they would sound like *puce*.
    Whoever drives this car is shopping for groceries
and aerosol spray, or now standing in line choosing
    between Doublemint and miniature Chicklets,
no one you'd recognize as individualist, creative thinker,
    rabid consumer of ozone-destroying products—
hairspray, bug spray, foot spray,
    carpet cleaner, tile cleaner, oven cleaner,
although the car's floor does not suggest
    someone especially concerned with cleanliness:
candy wrappers, loose change, a torn and stained map
    from a trip long, long ago.
Whoever drives this car has seen many things,
    perhaps too many.

As she stands in line, she might reflect upon one of them
    except that she is not given to reflection,
believes it's not all it's cracked up to be, this business
    of the interior. She knows it's possible, after all,
to get carried away, to realize you can't let go.
    Before you know it, you drive your obsession everywhere.
Meanwhile, in the parking lot, there is a woman
    leaning close to the maroon station wagon,
counting the number of plastic tops glued to the hood
    and it is changing her forever, she wants to believe.
She knows there are chance encounters
    that can steer your life into another direction
or awaken inside of you the life gone dull, rusted.
    You can see something once and never be the same,
although you cannot will this, nor will it away.
    Magnificent, she thinks. *Bread*, she thinks.
Milk for tomorrow.

Goddess Gone Fishing

Teresa Marta Costa

I feed the fish
handfuls of cat chow
& watch them scamper
    & dance.
They linger awhile
then skit, bouncing
off waters surface.
Fish like their treats
    soggy.
Dive in, feed upon it.

I skirt along the outer
edges watching new growth
    arrive.
New fish babies & mermaids
I find bear droppings an old
coyote den, once housing a
scowling lot of hungry cubs.

I catapult multitudes of
energy & await as the Goddess
sets up her fish pole.

Untenanted

Enid Dame

Standing over
Your uninhabited body,
Father,
I kept thinking,
"The building is still there."

I could picture it: the five floor Bronx walk-up
where memory started, for you.
For fifty years, you built and rebuilt it
until it seemed real as my skin.

Leaving you,
I enter your city
on a Greyhound bus.
There, I live quietly
among ghosts
I recognized from your stories.
Some rode the D-train all night.
Some wore fur coats in the Automat.
Some drank tea out of glasses and stared into space.
Some hung on my wall.

One wet spring
you came to see me.
I showed you the ocean at the edge of my block.
We stood and watched it, a caged animal,
shrunken, grey, talking to itself.
A police car crawled down the boardwalk,
rain-battered, slow as an insect.
"The city is dying," you said.

When we found your building,
you were disappointed.
Your mother's curtains were torn down.
Nobody spoke your language.

Still, it was there,
claiming its square of the Bronx. All around
gaping holes where houses had been:
yanked up like teeth,
burnt down to their roots,
half-collapsed,
doorframes hanging, rooms exposed
like body parts in a child's instructional toy.

You said, "This is awful. Let's go"
I thought, "At least it's standing.
People, families live here.
That counts for something. Doesn't it?"

Enid Dame

We could have touched its brick sides.
They would have felt hard, yellow, ordinary.
I could have touched you hand.
We could have gone in, found your mother's door,
felt for mezuzah lumps under layers of paint,
tried to ask questions.

We didn't. We went back to my place,
the crooked streets, the grumbling ocean.
You said, "I shouldn't have come."

When you were dying, in another city, I was in the next room,
on the phone, arguing with a nurse.
She didn't believe what was happening.

And when I touched you
finally
you felt hard, untenanted,
yet warm,
a brick wall
still holding the sun.

The Best Education

Alec Emerson

    I.

I was at Harvard,
taking Chemistry 20.
Down the corridor, a professor
worked to make napalm stickier.
The Vietnamese had learned to
scrape it off their pajamas.

Dow Chemical wanted an improved product.
The professor worked,
diligently, to improve the
torch of liberty,
and finally got it right,
so it would burn
to the bone.

ALEC EMERSON

II.

The telephone rang.
It was my mother, breaking.
A body bag
was coming home.

Villard de Honnecourt

Staats Fasoldt

I remember most the
Chartres Cathedral Bowling Team
its glory and colorful presence

you could rent shoes
near a former baptistery
where
legend said Charlemagne
stood

the Parisian bowling elite
came to roll
Jacques Tati
had a locker in the reliquary
as did Moreno the hairless
mexican

from the Clearstory
you could observe all
18 lanes
they were oiled
hard wood
with a soft

glow
not the polymer composite
used at Notre Dame

a pizza oven and Algerian
vendor stood
where Mary once gave
blessings

Mary
is the soul
in which the anointed
can be born
a true virgin
birth in attention

there is a small alter
near the north facade
where Mass is still given
at Easter
apparently written
in the lease
that they could continue to do so

new signs are up
in the tap room
a small green one that says
"league play after seven"

tables with red checkered
clothes
and small candles

against
damp stone walls

a sandwich
or some wings with
blue cheese and beer
could many times
lift my soul
on a dark
French February
night

Uth and Erhard were sipping mead at the bar
Erhard displaying a fierce countenance
as he sometimes did

there are so many ghosts
here
now celts
for on this spot their great tree
stood
cut down by Bishop Quintus
but whose
roots run deep
and exist
even
today

The Concierge of Hell

Howard Good

My father, suddenly aged,
works ghostly sums in his head,
the number of houses on fire,
the number of bones in the casket.
Pills don't seem to help;
whether face up or face down,
the cards leave the same puddles
of shadow on the table.
"Y is a crooked letter," he says
to the man in the tailored suit
who radiates a strident bonhomie
like the concierge of hell.
The windows run with rain,
though the air itself is fiery dust.
I look up at the sound, using my finger,
tender where I nicked it yesterday
with a knife, to mark my place.

Sorrow's Rooms

Howard Good

The room where the deserter exchanges clothes with me,

the room where the window looks out on silence,
the room where the radio plays your parents' wedding song,

the room where the shadows hatch like spider eggs,
the room where the children we once were are still crying,

the room where the woman licks the salt off words,
the room where the ocean seeps under the door,

the room where the dead glumly empty their pockets,
the room where the executioner's ax leans against the wall,

the room, the one you're in, where nothing ever happens.

Paris: Where All Thursdays Go to Die
after "Black Stone Lying on a White Stone"
by César Vallejo

Anne Gorrick

I will have died in Paris
more than one rainy day could remember the days
    already written in me
Paris, where all Thursdays go to die
Because today writes down these lines
solitary on this bone road

One rainy day could already point out the days left in me
I will look at today as if Thursday died in Paris
I will cross the street to avoid a Thursday
recluse from rain and bone

The rain could already underline the days in me
I regard Thursday as if it died in Paris
Thursday set the bones in my arm against the river
bones inaccurate inside
César Vallejo is stenciled in rain

The women are dead in Paris today
I have already emphasized the days that have cared for the I
Today is Thursday in Paris dying
Because the famous today, Thursday, exists entirely of
Vallejo's arm bones

Paris, a city in elegy
Finally there is no other side to this day
The woman, the field, the place that intersects last in work
Perhaps Thursday
Already anxiety in pleasure and work
The I against Paris
Eight of the bones in my arm make up this line
The death fact peels around the lower part of difficulty
The reign of bone, eight roads secluded in Thursday

Paris comes in bone at this moment
crossing in César Vallejo, tin plated, done
in ruptured "Oh" within this river Styx, this road
The way Thursday isolates the rain from bone

Mad Evil Times

Sari Grandstaff

We're incognito, out of earshot
disguised as flies by night
revealed as high-heeled by day
up, up and away
under your clothes
mothballroom dancers, light on our toes
falling in love in droves

itchy from circus knives,
scratch-off lives
in shining armor, enamored
at this dock, tick tock
happy hourglass tinks
we head off to our shrinks
our soft, comfy meds
hair locked up in dreads
buoys and girdles right this way
ship-shape, red tape
you lick my nape
ocean of chopsticks
sidekicks to tell your future

sew up your suture
it's aperture hour, sweet tarts are sour
no choice meet and greet
we're hidden, unbidden
we come, we stay
out in the open, guaranteed off
stay the course, code remorse
dot dash dot dash
the fight stuff, play rough
and tumble dry low
Can Buddhists wear permanent press?
give me your e-mail address
your snail mail, your hunky dory
mourning gory
read your robbed time story
of nights in shining paramour.

Something

Eamon Grennan

Something to do with how raindazzle at cloudbreak
Touches up three apples in their skins and makes them blush
Teal, cinnabar, gamboge; something with how that swan

Stands splayed on slime-covered stones at Claddagh-mouth,
A lovely alien; the cormorant speeding downstream has
Something to do with it, taking advantage of the Corrib's

Last mad dash for the sea, scattering black-headed, crack-
Voiced gulls, keen gliders, eyes like needles in their search
For scraps, casual vigilantes of anything out of the ordinary

Run of things on the river; and something about how
Those clouds pack their massy granite granaries with light—
Makes me ask what law in physics keeps these bottles

And bits of chipped wood in the turbulent trough
Of the small waterfall spinning and spiraling, fleeing
In circles, going nowhere: however far they fling

Themselves in the roil and roaring foamburst, they're
Caught and drawn in, at once fugitive and centripetal,
Stuck where they are while something in them seems

EAMON GRENNAN

A big breathless thrusting out that won't give up
The struggle, though it avails nothing, simply brings all
Back where it began, dizzy with longing, starting over

Again, and again over again, as if it meant something.

Innocence of Things

Eamon Grennan

Driving north. Shivers of valediction.
Tweed-folds of the Catskills in abrasive light;
Risen flame of a redtail riding a thermal;
Two geese through blue immensity. Sun

Scribbles its calligraphy of angle-spines
And snag-arms. All the dead leaves
Up again, jigging and reeling from
This brash wind scatter. The barred

Tail of a raccoon shimmers a little
In breeze-flutter. Rest of him sprawled
Still as stone on the road's shoulder.
Drip of fresh meltwater off a snowbank

Is the tick of the clock this March day
Moves to, slow as moss-ooze. Brazen
Daylight; acres of snow under a sky
Of sapphire; and I'm remembering

My old friend's fine old hands
As she held the fork steady, snail-slow,

Tendering a curl of baby corn
To her mouth, and I want to set her

Next to the innocence of things
As they stand up in frailty and fortitude
To light, and take its daily measure—
Their secular selves singular and glowing.

      (In memory of Phoebe Palmer)

I Give You Birth

Carol Graser

I give you birth under fat black sky
    heavily salted

I give you birth in palm of all mothers
    seat of explosion
    peppercorn crunched in the mouth

I give you birth before the sun's heat has gathered
    before the slant rays can dry her grasses

I give you birth beneath thin canopy of branches
    rocky tumult of debris
    decay's rough turn to abundance

I give you birth in cave of all voices of labor
    poetry carved
    in every word of all tongues
    chant of vast rhythms echoed in rounds

I give you birth like a diamond stolen
    retrieved from dumb finger
    brought back to earth's vein

I give you birth traveling the ticking gears of clocks
    having learned that hair raising
    tightrope walk
    I arrive at your perfect click

I give you birth clinging to the mane of one
    among stampedes of horses
    my blood is the sound of rushing forward
    my face rests on the sweating neck of speed

I give you birth as I've been your vessel
    as I've been your ocean
    your distance crossed

I give you birth onto woven hammock of patient
    impatient arms   your cheeks
    have been shaped to their kiss

I give you birth in anonymous rooms
    hotel furniture
    sheets of no smell

I give you birth among green gowned strangers
    TV tilted
    catching our view

I give you birth beneath crush of hospital layers
    doctors   administrators   insurance   the state

I give you birth in avalanche pocket
    we come howling mystery
    our voice stains the air

CAROL GRASER

I give you birth gray rain pummeling ground
   breaking deluge
   pelting dissolve

I give you birth undertow of contractions
   seized by the waist
   there is no shore

I give you birth undeniable sinking
   salty beginnings
   breath of each cell

I give you birth grunting push of sloth woman
   belly deep chanter
   O Anti Demure

I give you birth catch emerging black haired head
   slippery to hands
   that have dried from such water

I give you birth cradle you finally
   wet cheek sogs blessing my breasts
   I am fallen to small-lipped depths
   swallowed by sweet mouth of newness

The Weight of Snow

Don Haynie

It's almost silent,
just a faint whisper:
Steady, implacable, relentless,
the weight
accumulates. Time
is very much a partner in this
process. You
look once and the trees are
gently frosted, as though
some confectioner wished
to outline their forms
in white, the bare
branches starker than ever,
the evergreens looming
through the daylong dusk
darker, with an amplified power.
But the boughs begin to bow:
You look again, and the weight of age,
of ages, leans,
strokes them toward the ground,
like a heavy hand on a cat's
back, the shoulders
of the spruces slumped

Don Haynie

as if to say "enough!",
but there is more; and then
the rifle shots, the crack of limbs
whose weaknesses have been
found out. So we age too,
almost imperceptibly until
the sudden loss,
some major branch.

Books

Mikhail Horowitz

Bound objects, old kegs sweetening
Brains, opening ontological knots, spiny
Blossoms of our knowledge, shelves
Boldly offering Orientalism, Kabbalah, sex,
Baseball, ornithology, Ovid, Kallimachos, Samuel
Beckett, O'Brien, O'Neill, Kierkegaard, Shakespeare,
Blood Oranges, Omoo, Kabloona, Story
(Baby!) of O, Kaddish, Shogun,
Book of Obadiah, Koran, Susan
Brownmiller, Orwell, Omar Khayyam, Saul
Bellow, Oz, Olympus, Karl Shapiro,
Briggflatts, Odyssey, Odyssey (Kazantzakis), something
By Oates, Olson, Kafka, Sartre,
Bringing others orchids, kisses, stars.

Morgan

Mikhail Horowitz

Stroking her I could be stroking the Bayonne Tapestry,
its vatic comet above the battle summoned by thumbs
   in static of crackling fur

She is at least that old, and possibly older —
domesticated in Egypt, purring toy of Ptolemaic tots

An ancient art, to stalk a bird
To rend with joy the morning's immediate mouse

And she, too, will go the way of the Ptolemies, the Pharaohs,
   the blackest and bluest of Nubians;
a mummified hairball in the House of Bast, an ivory whisker
   in the scales of Mayet

this prelapsarian cat in my lap
already a dapple of calico dust.

Konghuin (a tune for the lyre)
an excerpt

translated by Heinz Insu Fenkl

Though I begged you not to cross the river,
You have gone to the other side;
Now that you have drowned, my love,
What shall I do, all alone?
      – Yo Ok
        (8th Century, Ancient Choson)

Translator's note:
Early one morning, Yo-ok's husband, Kwak Yi Cha-ko, was rowing across the river. On the bank he saw a woman trying to restrain her husband, a white-haired old man, who was trying to jump into the river. She could not stop him—he leapt in, swimming fiercely like a madman, but alas, he was swept away and drowned. The woman, in her grief, followed her husband into the water, singing a mournful song and playing the konghu. She, too, drowned. When Yo-ok heard this tale from her husband, she was so moved that she set the old woman's words to music and played it on her own konghu. Though there is no original text of this poem in Korean, there are copies that survive in the Chinese. It is said that the great T'ang poet, Li Po, inspired by Yo-ok, also composed a poem on the theme of "Konghuin," which is a generic term often translated as "lyre tune." According to some Korean scholars, "Konghuin" is the oldest surviving Korean poem from the Choson era.

Grieving for Yin Yao
Wang Wei (701-761 A.D.)

translated by Heinz Insu Fenkl

How long is a man's life
Before he returns to emptiness?
As I think of you, on the verge of death,
10,000 things trouble my heart.

Your mother not yet buried,
Your daughter only ten,
And yet from the far, cold, wilderness,
Already the sound of mourning.

Clouds drift across an empty sky
And songless go the birds in flight;
The way of the wanderer is lonely—
Even the sun sets pale and cold.

I am sorry—when you lived
And asked me to explain the dharma,
My teachings came too late.
In the end it was all vanity.

Your old friends have brought you gifts,
But mine were too late for you in life;
I have failed you in so many ways,
I weep and close my gate of twigs.

April 1968

Kate Hymes

Red azaleas blazed. Dogwoods bloomed white
four-petal-crosses past the Greyhound bus windows
as Mama and I rode, New Orleans to Atlanta,
that April. Mama said, "They crucified Jesus

on a dogwood." How could they have –
so frail, so delicate to bear all that weight.
Mama said, "God stunted the once mighty tree,
then redeems it each spring with remembrance."

The night before on TV we saw cities
burn. Mama and I wore black
arm bands. As we rode, we watched
azaleas and dogwoods in riotous

celebration bear witness:
stones still roll away.

The Seminar

Kate Hymes

Iron shackles clanked
onto the table. Placed among
books and papers, rough metal
smothered musings, silenced

pens scratching for understanding.
Iron gave weight
to studied words about
whips and chains and runaways.

Bulk made light
pursuit of metaphor and simile.
Passed from hand to hand,
each left and right

a balance pan lifting
the shackles up and down
to gauge their heft. Fingers
rubbed the biting metal.

Touch taught
what words could not,
how the soul
wears raw.

A perpetual caravan
of red and ragged
flesh moves confined
through time and space:

shuffle aboard slave ships,
stumble in coffles sold deep south,
shamble in chain gangs along dusty roads,
step aboard downstate busses for upstate prisons.

Barrier Canyon Style

Mike Jurkovic

"I will astonish Paris with an apple"
Cezanne boasted.
And I thought
"Okay,
 I'll try a peach.
 And if not a peach
 A pear.
 And if not a pear
 Then what?
 Plum? Night shade? Tomato?"

If art, like water, like war
Has no constant form
Then praise be
The nomads of Barrier Canyon,
Ancients chewing
Red ocher juice
To spit the Holy Ghost
With tongues afire,
Onto the climbing sandstone.

Imagine their need to astonish, to express,
Then bring into your own life:
Each day a mountainous palette
Blushed with blood,
The tincture of your heart.

Cattle Map

Mike Jurkovic

Don't you find it
The least bit preposterous
To assume you know the pickpocket
Because he reminds you of someone
You dated in high school?

How far out on a limb
Do you care to dangle,
Before dead weight
Snaps your perch
And they chopper you from the chasm?

Isn't there something
You wish to bestow
Exceeding your briny spoor?
Muttering about our cargo culture
With accusations on your lip.

Tell me something of your journey,
Give me something to help me through.
Aside from the standard cattle map
For a dollar at the door.

The Skies In Their Mouths

Christine Boyka Kluge

The skies in their mouths
meet in a kiss.
Hot and cold breath swirl,
lips unfurl and billow.
A summer storm
builds between them,
crackling.
Horizontal lightning
paints their tongues
orchid and gold.
Their single world is sealed.
It tastes of rain and torn petals.

Self-Improvement

Frank LaRonca

"I wasn't always so erudite. For example,
    when I was younger, there was this shyness
that gave me years with myself
    some people never have."

As he seduced his postal worker,
with whom no greater mail fraud
would ever be attempted,

these words sprouted unironically
about injustice. The final puzzle piece

morphed into just one more random
atom, impossible to get a fix on.

In an epiphany, he saw the metaphors
being created before the living
creatures could fulfill them.

He realized the folly of trying to find meaning
in a world where patterns of habit trumped
qualifiable observation and invention every time.

Frank LaRonca

Sure, last week he woke three days in a row
before his alarm could rouse his drowsy family

from their much different dreams of breakfast options,
but this was exceptional, proving nothing more

than that his bladder wasn't the vessel it used to be.
That a certain anxiety still gnawed toward fulfillment,

and though he hated the idea of self-improvement,
he did wish to recognize

the reflection in the hallway mirror
as one he used to love in the future.

The Ginger Jar

Sharmagne Leland-St.John

After you left,
Peter found
a large, glazed,
antique,
kaolin,
Chinese ginger jar
while rummaging
in the attic
next door.

With his long,
spidery,
flamenco fingers
he "gingerly"
passed it down
the ladder
to me.

Beneath the glaze,
painted orchids
grow on thin stems,

while butterflies dance
an erratic
pleine aire ballet.

Three handles
protrude,
sculpted,
then coiled
in the image
of three golden snakes,
guarding
some ancient treasure

From the imitation,
cut crystal vase,
I moved your bouquet
of fragrant freesia,
mixed in with
the serrated,
glossy
green leaves,
on sturdy stalks,
and the feathery,
small white,
(as yet)
unidentified
blossoms,
into the ginger jar

I tenderly
rearranged them
then placed it

"feng shui"
upon its own
inverted image
on the polished,
Louis quatorze,
mahogany table
where we three
had shared
so many
candlelight,
exotic,
gourmet,
midnight
meals.

They make
a whole new statement.
I wish
he had found it
before you left.

Twilight

Donald Lev

Dearest. The rainbow collapsed today.
No one had been riding it thank goodness.
I have negatives soaking in my darkroom
in a solution of tears and acid
that is no solution and will beget
no positives. In one of these negatives
You may be said to be silhouetted
against an empty sky. We shall see.

Don't dread anything. From point of view
of nothingness even vision farthest
back in the mind is no starting point.
Red letter days come and go to be sure.
Our transports seem to flow, but are mostly bleak
The photos show, & recede like winter.

Receding. A hair line. A shoreline.
A breathline. A heartline. My palms turn upward,
then backward to cover my eyes. It is
a gesture the meaning of which I
am uncertain. There are no thoughts behind
the covered eyes when I do this. Only

DONALD LEV

a sense like the sound of a river
entering an unquiet harbor.

Listen. You can hear laughter in the waves
as being is transformed into memory;
as when a father dies or a wise word
is recorded for posterity.

Scene from a Marriage

Donald Lev

So precarious!
Two tipsy piles of books
At the edge of the dresser,
Her reading glasses tucked
In between them.

On my side,
An even tipsier pile
Threatens from the night table.

Autistic Superkid

Brian Liston

I am and have always been
The autistic superkid
I am one of the first
But not the last
And I am always trying to improve
I am an ambassador of two worlds
Half-citizen of Earth; Half citizen of Wallbrook
This is how I truly am
Even though it's not how I look

What I Ate

Valerie Martin

The food I had alone:
Bread, tea,
Then, with friends:
Fish, bread.
At dinner, unexpectedly
More friends:
Beans, rice, salad, wine.
Later, at home:
Chocolate cookie, more wine.
All this food, heavenly food
In one day, with no effort. And now this, now this:
Coffee, bread, half an apple.
So much food in one day,
And with each bite
The pleasure of solitude and food,
Of friendship and food,
No thought of sorrow,
Of dry bread,
Of the dead,
Fed on the tears of the living.

You Found Her

Valerie Martin

It was a seizure.
Your cousin saw her,
Running into the corn.
You were the youngest,
Too young, you were ten,
 Your uncle cried:
"She'll freeze to death."
It was Nebraska.
No one asked you, you didn't say, "I'll help."
Everyone rushed from the house
And you went too, running hard between the brittle rows,
Tall, taller than you. This corn was dead already.
The sun was setting; you could see your breath.
Your hands were numb; you'd forgotten your gloves,
And you found her.

Was she alive?
I asked twenty years later,
When you told this story
Over coffee in Styrofoam cups.
Outside it was the University and 100 degrees.
You were a painter; you painted clouds,
Canvas after canvas, nothing but the sky.

Three years later you quarreled with your wife.
She stormed out.
You put a shotgun barrel in your mouth,
Pulled the trigger with your toe.
You were barefoot.
I don't know who found you.

Grand Central - Passing Through on the Way Home after a Long Day

Karen Neuberg

Descending into Grand Central's enormous scale and din during late rush-hour
weeknight, I force pause in the great concourse while trying to remain

out of the way of those intent and bustling. For a moment, it's mine to feel
the great space having its way with me, and I'm small beneath night sky

that graces the entire ceiling. I sense enclosed space so huge
it catches sound and body and whooshes them away. My body doesn't mind.

I'm in another era, as time-and-passages before speak from within enclosed expanse.
The great zodiac looks down – seven constellations. I locate Orion and Pegasus,

Betelgeuse and Aldebaran, until the swirling around my stiff neck makes me aware
I'm dizzy and feel like a gaping tourist. I begin to walk, still glancing up,

wishing the bulbs behind the pinholes were bright enough to shine
    out as stars
in a clear-night, Hudson Valley sky. I warp and weft as called for,
    part of a tapestry

continuously replaced by a newer weave. I'm heading for the
    subway now, intent
as I pass sweeping staircases where a sign informs of a special
    event and chamber

music drifts almost soundlessly my way. Side shops are busy,
    selling fish to radishes.
I slow at temporary columns of 9/11 photos and read—"missing",
    "we'll always

love you"... — then enter into my last challenge here tonight—the
    crowded corridor
and escalator to the subway lines. I cut across the petals of the
    compass rose

just barely noting my direction on earth's surface as I rush to catch
    my ride toward home
so far away from me that I'll ask where I've been all day upon my
    own return.

Shooting Star

Robert Polito

"I seen a shooting star tonight, and I thought of you..."

In a San Francisco basement apartment
There's a woman I keep hearing about, who
Claims for the last twenty years she's lived
With Bob Dylan, and wishes to write a book about it.
That might mostly be new to him – *hey man,*
You must be putting me on. But she sells scarves
From her own North Beach shop, and according
To this woman Dylan's changed – a lot –
Heavy now, yet kind, if also a little
Crazy, in and out of hospitals, he doesn't look
Like himself. Still, wherever he travels
He mails her love poems in his familiar
60's style, and she'd be honored to show them around.

A sleepy kitchen at dawn, the woman steps
Towards the kettle, pajamas open to her waist,
An owlish man, drunken, slothful, lags behind.
The glamour of the damaged, but how much
More gratifying for her not to have spun the whole

ROBERT POLITO

Hazy farrago out of loneliness, madness, or for money,
And this morning to wake beside someone
Who persuades you he recorded "Shooting Star" just for you.

Three Horse Operas
for Patti Smith

Robert Polito

At the end of Bing Crosby's *Riding High* his horse
Will be buried in the clay of the racetrack where he fell,
As a lesson for all of us. Sad, waggish Bing,
The Mob didn't want Broadway Bill to win, so the jockey
Pulled on the reins until the thoroughbred, straining
Over the finish line first, collapsed, heart attack.

I loved you like a guitar string breaking
Under the conviction of a clumsy hand–
Something like that... I suppose I must have
Been thinking of you and your complex and beautiful band,
Except the image demands I hold the guitar,
If not you, and the broken string, as

Over and over loudspeakers call riders to the starting gate.
The track bartender and a teller, a sharpshooter and
    the chess master
Wrestler, the petty con man and a cop, reprise their parts.
The heist gang dons clown masks, and
Sherry will betray George, and Johnny can't love Fay,
And the fortune in the suitcase just blows away.

Freight Trains

Marilyn Reynolds

Flat on my back
they crisscross my sticky naked body
every Indiana summer night
The whistles and head beams blind my dreams
pulling me into consciousness to push them back
where they belong

You were a hot musician
raising your trombone to the treetops
dedicating your soulful offering to me
that steamy afternoon
In that memorable forest of dripping greens
you leaned your lanky body against a sycamore tree
promising
I'll be back to find you

All that summer
you hopped freight trains in a jig-saw puzzle pattern
around the mid-west up towards Chicago
where foundry smoke
thickened the soupy air
streaking past cool water-ways
and serpentine waves of dunes

catching the night train
moving north

Each time you entered a boxcar
you knew you were trespassing
when the hobos fell silent
A man of privilege you took out your shiny horn
asking their permission to play
You had a way of splicing music with smiles
soon instruments with stories to tell
surfaced from pockets and beds of straw
shy smiles broadened into grins
as the jamming traveled into the night
mellowing with pastel chords of dawn

You wrote me every day
once from Reynoldsburg Ohio
train doors open to summering countryside
barnyard smells and new mown hay
I could hear your trombone improvising
with west coast harmonicas
a thumb harp from St. Louie
mean sticks against floorboards
gritty blues from Virginia
fast moving concert with crickets
and heavy sleep sounds
picked up and challenged by the lone train whistle
unfolding a misty canopy of jazz
that hovered over the landscape
long after the train was out of sight

Dreamer dreamer up all night
I felt it all through your eyes keeping me awake
longing for your life

Back at college
unpacking my trunk
the news came over the radio

You'd been found beside the tracks
trying to hop a free familiar ride to school
the first image that flashed across my mind
was a bloody mangled mess of brass and flesh
your black rimmed glasses flung far into a field
among grazing spotted hogs
But in reality
you hit your head
and died instantly
trombone still encased
resting by your side

The night is choking with heat

The mournful whistle of a freight train
traverses this flattened land in a slow steady cadence
tripping-ever-so-lightly-on-the-game-board-edge-
of-the-slumbering-city-braking-at some dark crossing
screechingsteelagainststeel

Slitting the black sky with Silver blades of high C
Stabbing clean through my memories
to the tracks.

A Double Life

Tad Richards

I.

A young woman in love with deception
embarks on a double life.
She kisses her husband goodbye
each morning, leaves the house carrying
a mesh bag and meticulously printed list.

She goes to a rent-controlled apartment
on the upper West Side of Manhattan, where
the fireplace burns birch logs from the
Adirondacks, the ceilings have exposed
beams, the bookshelves signed first
editions, carelessly stacked: Celine,
Colette, Baudelaire, Valery, Ionesco. There,

she is 47 years old, and adept at treason.
She has sold industrial secrets to Japan,
Broadcast troop movements to the Viet Minh.
She has soft breasts, in this second life,
she is surprised at how heavy they are,
and how glad she is to shed them, when
she steals home in time to meet her young husband.

II.

One day a boy enters her flat.
She is wearing a slip the color of teeth,
she is reading a biography of Laval.
The boy is slight, his eyes are like skin.
He is the same age as her young husband from
her other life, and he has his own key.
He is her son.
      She wonders if a robe would
be apropos, but there's none at hand.
He seems not to care. He might be naked
himself: he walks with elbows crooked,
fingers splayed, touching nothing, not even himself.
He barely speaks. She sways as he walks,
as if she were rocking him. She asks
does he need money. He tells her
Soon, soon there will be money. Soon.
Vive la Falange, he murmurs to the shuttered window.

III.

She becomes obsessed with the parts of her body
she cannot see, first in her second life,
then in her first. It is close to the only
attribute her two lives have in common.
She asks her young husband to describe her back to her.
It is like flight, he says.
It is like landing, he says. Like a high tor
where eagles perch, like the deck of a carrier
where men scamper with flags and torches,

like a tiny rutted airstrip between two peaks
in the Andes, where gasoline fires blaze at night.

She asks one of her lovers to describe her ass to her.
He is an old, hard, black man, a Legionnaire,
veteran of Dien Bien Phu, and the battle
of Algiers. It is three hands across,
he says. I saw one like it in Tunis, on a whore.

IV.

A blind man jaywalking is the signal.
The *thwack* of his white cane on
her rear bumper, the *tick*
on the radiator of the Buick behind her.
She drives without looking back.
She has been told where to go, to a rendezvous
in Connecticut, with the man who is to become
her lover. She sees him
in front of a small country inn. He is larger
than her young husband, and casts a shadow
like the blackbirds of Connecticut.
He draws her to him, and she thinks *so this
is how another man kisses... take the
time to savor this, because it doesn't
come along too often in your life.*

But she pulls away.
She looks back once, to fix him
in memory, but she will remember
nothing. She drives, instead,

to a cabin in the Adirondacks.
Across the lake is a tavern,
accessible only by a small powerboat.
She crosses the lake at night,
sits in her boat beneath the window,
close enough so her face is lapped
by the blinking glow from the Utica Club
sign in the window, but she does not go in.

Conception

Cheryl A. Rice

Searching from darkness to darkness
in the back of my aunt's Bel Air.
It was May, forsythias popping kernels of flowers,
wet crickets tuning to the rhythm of the growing sun.
The beaches were still empty, save for
clamdiggers, metal detector retirees.
It is 1961, and Camelot is still a go.
Marilyn and Arthur are calling it quits.
A sperm searches in this dark certainty.
Explosion of rubber? Irresistible longing?
I am found, both halves of me,
by some divine crapshoot.

My molecules grew in terror.
Do not think I was unaware.
The agony of the hunt, the shotgun chapel,
it is all here somewhere, and I don't want to say
it burned a sort of nervous tattoo on my skin,
but I glow with an incandescent yelp
to a god who let them stumble,
with me as the fruit, into their own Eden
and toothmarks shaped my brain in such a way
as to make other mythologies

the stuff of Bugs Bunny cartoons.
They retired to oranges in their middle age.
All apples are poison to me now
unless boiled beyond recognition.

American Epitaphs

William Seaton

The Surfer

By a wave's glint
I flew. I leave
nothing. Know
I'm not at rest,
my parts now skim
a foreign sea-top.

The Farmer

For fifty years
I hauled good things
through grit and clod,
only now to slide so smoothly,
slip down earth's gullet

The Man of Business

Account book joys,
startles, disappointments
by which I beguiled time
and, it seems, time me:
now a box of broken parts,
      all glitter gone.

The Athlete

That boiling blood
that surged so glad
has ebbed and pooled
and fallen back
unable today to hold
the least little heat.

Boca de Tomatlan

William Seaton

From this cove the hills
swell up like old tumors,
straining with luxuriance,
tense with heat and damp
and pain of constant overreaching.
An iguana with a bad conscience
dashes down a tree and vanishes.
A bright orange flower offers
to sell herself to tourists.
A pelican bobs like a buoy.
Its ancient eyes assure
all who happen here,
"Have no fear. I, too,
am your heart's likeness."

The persistence of ashes

Kenneth Salzmann

In fact, it is the roses that remain.

They enter the house one by one all summer long,
and longer. I place them on the mantle beside the urn
where they will expend their pinks and reds petitioning
what gods they know for the persistence of your ashes.

And they will weep petals across the hearth.

At times, I catch myself believing in the immutability
of ashes, as if we are of this place or any other. As if
the generations that go on spreading like ash will turn
one day to the fixed notion of an unwavering place that is home.

The roses were planted fifty years ago or more, a neighbor said,
by a woman who went about, as people do, growing flowers
and growing old until there was nothing left but roses to testify
that she had ever been. And we set out to make a home amid the
    thorns
and petals of her life. We nested in the oak-lined rooms that
    remembered
all her moods and all her movements, but only briefly. And you
    took it upon

yourself to cleanse and nourish those roses, perhaps in hopes of
    sanctifying
a transitory life followed seamlessly by ash and bone.

My Mother's Owl Collection

Judith Saunders

These owls look well traveled,
a cosmopolitan bunch.
Peruvian plaster figurines
hunch beside far Eastern kin,
stylized owls in gold and black
(Taiwan's fine-wrought laquerware)
marching behind Latino birds
more daring in design, more
extravagant in hue. Owls
scarcely recognizable—
crudely rounded like homemade balls—
pose in neighborly nearness
to sculptures so exquisite
each feather stands erectly etched.

This international parliament
is a multi-media event:
porcelain vies with wood and clay,
marble with rubber and plastic,
paper mache with unknown stone.
The hollowed bodies of two Indian birds—

cardboard coated with shellac—
serve as boxes, their heads as lids.
Singly or in well matched twos and threes
they gather at their meeting ground,
this shelving big enough to house
an ever growing ethnic mix.

Sturdy or fragile, fierce or serene,
grave or fey, the migrants brood
and flap in silent amity.
A golden, Oriental owl shuts
one eye in wise, perpetual wink,
gloats in this reversal
of avian Diaspora
--divinely ordained, no doubt—
The world made whole
piece by piece: all owl.

The Weaver

Jan Zlotnik Schmidt

She traces
the outlines
of continents
Antarctica, Africa, South America,
    Asia, Europe
She runs her fingers along
lines of latitude
spider thread lines
silk black thread
like the waxed cord
that pulls stray hair
from the brow
or sews lips shut
or stitches the
hide of deer

Fine strong threads
dark and taut
stitch after stitch
of worlds

It is so easy
she thinks

Jan Zlotnik Schmidt

to trace a world
the frayed edge
of continents
the space of sea and land
the surface of water
the upside down Vs
that show the mountain ranges
the Himalayas, the Jura, the Tatras
So easy to imagine
desert plateau
and rough terrain
so easy to cup hands
full of blue air
palms open to the sky
and then press them down
down onto the flat spaces
the quiet places of this earth

Rivers and mountains rise and fall
fall and rise
under the tips of her
outstretched fingers

She pulls the thread
The world tightly
coiled around her thumb
now white as stone
And then she lets it go
The world unravels
dissolves into blue air

The measure of our uncast dreams

A Photograph of my Parents in the Catskills, Circa 1937

Jan Zlotnik Schmidt

He hams for
the camera
cigarette dangling
from his lips.

She smiles
a cherry
lipstick smile.

I stare into the picture
imagine thick summer air
honeysuckle and mock orange
light striking oak leaves
framing the shot.

And I wonder
When no one was looking
did he carelessly touch her wrist?
Did she lean towards him
eyes closed lips tight
holding back desire?
Did they whisper those
pleasantries only lovers know?

Jan Zlotnik Schmidt

And when did it change?
When did their smiles thin?
Their pulse slow?
When did sorrow add heft to their bones?
When did they fall to earth
and become my flesh and blood?

I squeeze between them
into a patch of light
A white leaf in the
dark background
of the shot.
I reach to touch them.
They vanish.
My body still unframed.

3 Poems

Sparrow

Group of A's

      A
  A   A
    A A
A

Softness

Softness
is my brother.

Rows

Rows
by any other name
would still be straight.

Ascension

Margo Stever

*It takes seven strong men to drag the six foot
heart of a blue whale across the deck of a
whaling ship.*
                    Faith McNulty

Beads of sweat well up on the sea-
stained faces of the seven men
who bear the still warm heart
of the blue whale to the boiling vats.
The men are deliverers; they tug,
rip, tear the heart
across the deck to the seething pots.
But their hands stick to surfaces
like flypaper, and recoil,
the red matter teething into fingers
as if leaching out the blood.
Ventricles, gaping mouths,
stand ajar; red smoke rises
in the darkening mist. Harsh wind
raps against crevices, something
trying to get back in,
tapping out an aberrant beat,
an unknown code, and something whines,

long and low, a sea moan.
Only a crane can lift
a six-foot heart, and as the last
inch of the raised organ
recedes into the stewing vats,
dismembered parts of the heart ascend
and billow over the deck.
Seven men inhale the vision, their hearts
slackening with each breath.

Conversation with Bertolt Brecht

Margo Stever

> *Solely because of the increasing disorder*
> *in our cities of class struggle,*
> *some of us have now decided*
> *to speak no more of cities by the sea,*
> *snow on roofs, women...*
>   *Brecht*

As if the Chilean songs of revolution
would bring back the gray fishing boats
sailing through frail, deepening waters
at dawn and the seagulls making earthly sounds.
As if these songs could restore the balance,
the driven leaf, nail old
and rusted, shoved through the bent bough.

Each step through mirrors brings us
back to the pitch of sleeplessness,
the unstrung dream, an oil slick
on an ocean still and black.
As if all the songs of revolution
could bring the murmuring tree back,
could restore wind to the rigging,
full sail to the morning light.

How many years, messages, wars,
strange incidences, ironies?
The wary eye of the mother
wanted to protect her child,
promise more, cities near the sea,
clear waters, full sail,
the morning light.

(excerpt from)
THE BORROMEAN ISLANDS
For the Posse

H. R. Stoneback

I. Isola dei Pescatori Variations

A. (Written at the Hotel Verbano* July 2000)

We must travel far until we come
to an island with no bridge, no cars;
it must be an island with a café
and no cars; let it have one small elegant
hotel with a fine waterfront restaurant;
let there be a ferry to transport us
to the mainland, if we must go across;
let us cherish the hour the ferry service
ends, the tourists all gone, the island ours
again; let this island with no cars be
a place where cats sun themselves on the docks,
strut unalarmed in the middle of what
passes for a street, and human footfall

---

*Toscanini's lakeside hideaway on Fishermen's Island,
where the portrait of the Maestro hangs in the lobby alongside
a framed copy of this poem.

in cobblestone lanes dictates the rhythms
of island life, as we stop in the middle
of any lane and salute the day's order
of things with cats and neighbors that we meet.

Let it be an island with no cars,
a café (where Frederic Henry and Hemingway
stopped), a well-run hotel clean and cheerful,
with all *les plaisirs de la table*
in the restaurant in the garden
on the terrace by the lake where we eat
four local fish courses caught by our
Fishermen's Island neighbors in the morning
sun, where even lake-loud comminatory Alps
do not disturb what the cats have to tell us
about fish and fishermen, about ourselves.

B. (Fishermen's Island, off Stresa: July 2000)

Up before the sun, walking and waking
island lanes, I stand on the lakeshore
and stare at far luminous hills where unknown
people lead secret lives of joy. Circling
the island I see many cats and women,
and three old men casting off in a fishing boat.
Where people still fish, most men rise early.
But it is mainly the women I see,
poised in ritual places the sun touches first,
gathering the sun, ripening, as if in some
fat mythical mountain vineyard.
Sudden fog rolls across the lake and burns
my throat like last night's grappa. Street cats gaze
at me, contemplating the Human Sphinx,

mesmerized by human multiplicity,
as I sing out loud and skip stones across
the lake. The cats do not regard me with
ironic eyes which see but have no vision,
which mock but never take possession.
How do they see me—am I inverted Film Noir?
And those mirror-jugs of water in doorways—
I thought they must be offerings to some Saint.
I asked the man at the store: "No, for the cats,
they see themselves, run, piss on some other door."

This island is a place to visit
in a dream, yet it exists everywhere
that it is, as quiet and real as the lake
is wet. The island is shaped like a fish.
By a strange lake you must empty yourself
for sleep (Darl says...My Island is the Fish).
The lake, the mountains, talk to me. The lake
prefers intimate forms of address,
but the Alps refer to themselves in
the third person. In the rhetoric
of lethargy, I compose myself
for the next sentence. Wind moans over the lake,
wavetones break, howl like vowels, consonants crash
on rocks, leaking lake-language secrets.
I write in my head a noise that rhymes
with Nature, with brooding on God and Time.
The lines I write all wind and lean toward love.
I watch a young girl lead an old man gently
down the lakeshore where he runs his hand
along an ancient fishing boat, rotting, half-sunk.

It is an island with an open heart.

I like the way the sun reaches into
alleys and crochets the green and red
fishing nets draped from staircases and porches;
I like the first sunlight spilled on the white
and yellow walls of red-roofed houses;
I like the way the spine of the fish,
the narrow main street, winds toward San Vittore,
the eleventh century church with the high
white steeple, and the fisherman's iconography
inside. I like the way the narrow side lanes
lead always to water, lake-and-mountain
views framed in stone; I like how it feels when
the first ferry comes and the last ferry leaves,
how the island returns to the Middle Ages.
Liking all this, the fishermen talk French to me.
All poets, all of us, long for a place
like this, a homeplace we have never known,
and we make in our songs the ghosts of the dead
we have never known, and we yearn to praise
a lost world that we never really had.
I do not seek the merely picturesque:
I walk the winding narrow street thinking
perhaps I will meet something quaint and old-
fashioned, like Marxism, like Surrealism.

III. Isola Madre

Vine-covered stone archway, ornate iron gate
frames a slice of ultimate blue lake;
winding paths among rare plants, trees, flowers—
peacocks and pheasants and parrots roam free.

Madre is a comfortable island,
a place you could live; the palace is small,
in perfect scale, a modest thirty rooms or so,
really just a country house, a place to live
in peace under soaring palm trees, the cashmere
cypress and, strayed from the Mediterranean,
lemon-scented Alpine groves and olives.

In the exotic woods we hear Church chimes
from somewhere across the lake, deep sound, wide
over water, rhyming with peacock cries.

We emerge into a clearing where parrots
call out our names. The lawn is lush with birds,
peacocks and pheasants, blue parrots in trees.
Feisty peacocks scream from a barn rooftop,
a pair of parrots chatter back, seem to mock
them, or us, as we sit to watch the birds.

We watch an old man gather peacock feathers
as they drift down from the roof; he collects
others from the ground, sits down on the grass,
leans back against a tree, gently arranges
the feathers on his lap. We wonder if he
is caretaker, gardener, tourist, or mystic.
He closes his eyes, seems to sleep. White screams
invade his dreams of numberless suns, God's
Eyes, and unicorn moons rise and ride his sleep.
Three white peacocks strut close to him, great tails
spread, study him with motionless regard.
At last they move when his body trembles,
perhaps surrendering to sleep, or the feathery

Tickle of Grace. Or both. The peacocks approach
us, web of a thousand eyes. We close our eyes,
listen intently in the deep dark where
all the bird-cries echo and sound the same
and we cannot say the sound of our names.

        ***

Sometime later, a peacock feather lands
on my hand, brushes me awake, thinking
of all things heard, seen, learned, and things unlearned,
how Grace and Mercy are always unearned,
how we had better move so we do not miss
the last crossing to Fishermen's Island.

Untitled

Christine Lilian Turczyn

On the field beyond my porch, deer gather
like sparrows of silence at the edges of guilt.
One leaves the herd, flies, like a promise briefly
remembered.
After the hedges shift, blue quiet settles in again.
It has been a long time since the deepest self
became a poem, lover, a familiar street. Ages, it seems
since we met, hands moving over braille of bodies,
reading what we could not speak, that you, a medic,
and I—broken—
could somehow drink deep water again.
How, when the world exploded around us?
When border deserts ran dry, women walked in heels
for work?
You carried me, as over
the river of my life.
"In case I had to," you said, and I wished
you could let go of Viet Nam.
I wished that we,
could fall through the rifts in our lives,
like tears, in this moment balanced,
between today and today,
this hush of deer,
waiting for rain.

Elements of Style

Pauline Uchmanowicz

What if poets had to pick? The ocean or the stars.
A reputation in truth telling or a prize in diplomacy?

Seabed or zodiac. Water or fire. Density or infinity.
There's travel by Chinese junk with shipwreck

Or space capsule disaster. Commerce or exploration.
Marine biologist or aeronautic engineer.

Dictating rhyme, form and meter it's either
Waves as repetition or constellations as pattern,

Tide and undertow or equinox and quasar.
Cardinal points and horizons stay in joint custody

And every bard gets clarinets, trees and the rigadoon.
Also Spanish butterflies, mountains and Dutch windmills.

Five-Minute Hamlet

Pauline Uchmanowicz

Flip-flops strike a sonata
on wet pavement
where rain has fallen

The hum of insects
filters the air.

Trees stand tall
like pillars in an opera house.

We do not want
our duet
to carry on dramatically—
no trickery
leading to ruin or death
waiting in the wings.

We won't compose
formal gardens,
listening for
each storm's coda:
branches thudding
down mown lawns.

A Valentine in Green Pastures

Bob Wright

I think that I shall love you till
the cows come home.

So if you were concerned
about the steadfastness of my
devotion, please rest easy.

Because those bovine creatures have been
lost for decades now, their herdsman
dead for years, their owner compensated
handsomely for their abrupt departure.
Because they've no intention of
returning. Have agreed among themselves
that it's more fun to clog up traffic on the major
thoroughfares than stand around some field
somewhere complaining that a Sunday painter
has not captured what they truly represent.

So let's forget the cows, as everybody
else has done who is not driving. It's love
we're speaking of. My love for you, which
will go on much longer even than it takes
for one of them to leap the moon.

Japanese Coasters

Robert H. Waugh

1 The Glass

Every afternoon, the catastrophe
of the day, I rest
a paper-thin glass upon
one of these faded coasters,
its stem
flutes to the petals of chill gin.

                             Geishas
and laborers, geishas
plucking at zithers and yellow fans,
at knots and ichthyphallic
pens, their accoutrements, kimonos
lush on their wrists
and aromatic pin-pricked mounds of hair.

                             The others
plod off to the yellow streets
uphill and downhill barren until
the chill night blows.

The narrow
noise of the heavy streets
and the pluck of the zither
soak through the room, I sip
their names, their doorways.

2 The Street

We lean narrow-roofed
and narrow-footed
striding uphill from the shore, we lean
halyards expressive
narrow-sailed out to sea.

This busyness
of the street walks you in, the perspectives
at a loss
leading you past the grills, the fowl
slung from the beams, the pots
steaming, the lazy succulence
of poppies.

But
narrow-paneled and narrow
cobbled departure oppresses us, we lean
off in three narrow ships
at the end of the sea.

3 Barrel-maker

He labors in the hoop, his knots of bone
and flesh stoop to the hoop, he wrenches
the ropes in an iron bar.

                      Atop his monkey-
masked top-knot Mount Fuji floats
at the peak of the sky encased
in the hoop, it does not touch
the hoop but
huddles across his back.

                      His shoulders lean
to the hoop, the mallet rocks
on his knee, its mass outbalances
the mountain but between them,
mallet and mountain,
they circle the hoop, the ferocity
knotted against the man's
scant hair and knobby ears.

4 The Bridge

You cannot see either bank, the rain
clatters upon the boards
of the high bridge, the strokes of the rain
slash through your breast.

                      The framework
criss-cross and knotted

shudders against the river blows,
against the deeps and shallows
roiling and knocking.

                But we
bend to the rain, we hurry
firm-footed beneath our loads, a narrow-
banked raft skims beneath us
but either
bank lies beyond us, and either
bank is the end of the world.

5 The Writer

The stroke of her eye, the stroke
of her yellow sleeve that drapes
her tablets, the stroke
of her narrow pen inhibits and regards
the script.

        A squiggle
that should be a pen-rest turns out
its snail horns to her.

               A black sleeve arched
and curlicued in chalk-
blue brambles
the knot between her eyes, her chin
elaborates each slant
choice.

      She ruffles
the papers in her hand,
the knot between her eyes stares blank
far away from them,
an unbearable russet
burns at her wrist.

            A window
lets down a narrow sun.

6 The Sea

The fingering wave
lingers, a precipice of fingers
lurching to fall on our narrow-
bladed skiff.

          In the center
of this construction Mount Fuji
as though it were a wave
hovers to sweep
us off.

        Each wave
sweats an ungainly snow,
our labor
in the mountains unfaced,
our rudder, our keel, our prow
drawn forth
beneath the exquisite fall
of the waves to the rim of elsewhere.

7 The Two Bridges

The yellow and broad sun
upon us, we shuffle
taking the arch of the first bridge,
our feet slap.

        In knots at the toll-gate
horned merchants commiserate
and urge us on, the sun
urges us on, the boards beneath our feet
settle and arch, the spring
of the day takes us on, above us
banners on pikes or heads
celebrate the sky.

        Then the second bridge
arches footloose
to the arched laborious sun,
our backs arched to that
knot in our shoulder-blades.

        Burdens
brown and four-square stretch
across the arch, our faces
ache in the weight.

        Baskets
and buckets trudge off upstage,
we pray that we may someday
trudge off upstage, but the inch of it
lies in eternity.

8 The Cartouche

In each of these prints, high up
indefatigably hung in the sky
an elegant scribble pronounces
upon this labor.

            I lift
my glass from the coaster
transfixed by the knots, the thrang
biceps and fingers,
those abstruse sigils my cold glass
blots out.

          Cool skies
utter a primal word
and the deep blue waters or else
the bottom line of the print
a primal word as I lift
my careless extravagant glass.

                     The word
hangs stricken, hooking
and gouging your eye, it lifts
a blood-gorged sun to unsay us,
it flutters and steeps.

Popinjay in the Japonica

Sarah Wyman

Dame Elaine shined silver, wore lace, and painted teacups.
Some decades past, wrapped in cream satin, with orange
blossoms in her hand, she'd made a match with a Rock-
erfeller, his family mansion, the vast grounds.
I, the gardener, enter the picture, a fly
on the wall, tending the boxwood, pruning this tree

or that. My quiet life on the estate, country
calm after city living, pleases me. A cou-
ple of marriages taxied by like butterflies.
More than ornamental cabbages, or orange
rays of sunset dropping their warmth on the ground,
I like to think and watch my thoughts take off like rock-

ets in a spacious place. *She* sits on her rock-
er, doing just what I do, counting seams on trees,
conversing with bees, shaking cold coffee grounds
into the leaves. But Dame isn't the same, her cup-
id's bow lipstick awash in tears, her brow an orange
wedge of worry, and every birthday Shoo-Fly

pie comes out burned, since the night I watched her hope fly
out the window. She saw a boy atop a rock,

standing bright, steady and still as a lighted an-
gel. He took aim and shot at a spreading tree,
knocking her popinjay from its japonica.
(*Please* don't tell I saw her bird hit the ground.)

In a Picasso confusion of form and ground,
tears melted the colors and quince, her high flier
was dead: split beak and his broken body now cup-
ped in her hands. She buried him under a rock,
patting the earth with her pink Pappagallo, tre-
mendously moved by the last feather, torn orange

aflutter, as it fell on the fresh grave, arranged
with trefoil and leftover lilies. Her heel ground
a hole as she rose and spun 'round to scan the trees.
She did not spot me, only a lost lonely fly
catcher hunting for nest sites or bugs, rock to rock.
When Dame Elaine sees me nights now, I lift my cup

up to her (always alone), rocking in her cup-
ola, orange ground around the japonica tree.

Author Biographies

Barbara Adams has published two books of poems, *Hapax Legomena* and *The Ordinary Living*, a book of literary criticism, *The Enemy Self: Poetry & Criticism of Laura Riding* and poems, essays and stories in journals and anthologies. Her play, *God's Lioness & the Crow: Sylvia Plath and Ted Hughes*, was first produced by Mohonk Mountain Stage Company. She was Professor of English and Director of the Business Communication Program at Pace University, and is now retired to write full-time.

Jacqueline Renée Ahl had her poem, Memories, published in Mohonk Mountain Stage Company's *Vanguard Voices of the Hudson Valley – Poetry 2007*. She recorded *Underdog Lovely, Selected Poems 2001-2005* and has been the featured poet at numerous local readings. Her play, *Fear Itself*, was awarded Best New One-Act of 2005 by the Brevard Little Theatre, NC. She is currently the Specialist for Disabilities and Learning at SUNY New Paltz. and an instructor for the Summer Institute for the Gifted at Vassar College.

Jay Albrecht started writing in 1953, from simple quatrains about the sea, to haikus, to internally-rhymed lyric verse on everything from nature to relationships. Now some 250 poems, many in anthologies, journals and periodicals published in NYC, Westchester and Sweden: *Voyager, International Voices, Mensa Journal, New York Magazine* plus two chapbooks. He reads at arts groups and at twelve Westchester non-profits with the Poetry Caravan. He is an engineer, copywriter, psychologist; now artist, chaplain, and activist.

Kat Alexander, originally from Manhattan, lives in New Paltz. She was first published at age 13 in *Read Magazine* for winning first prize in the Ann Arlys Bowler competition. A graduate of SUNY New Paltz, she was the 2005 winner of the Tomaselli Prize in poetry and was awarded the Thomas Elliot award upon graduation.

Roberta Allen has authored eight books, including the story collections *Certain People* and *The Traveling Woman*; a novella, *The Daughter*; the novel, *The Dreaming*; and the memoir, *Amazon Dream*. She teaches at the New School and has taught at Columbia University. A conceptual artist as well, she has exhibited worldwide with work in the collection of The Metropolitan Museum.

Jacob M. Appel, a native of Scarsdale, New York, has taught most recently at Brown University in Providence, Rhode Island, and the Gotham Writers' Workshop in New York City. His fiction has appeared in *Alaska Quarterly Review, Colorado Review, Missouri Review, North American Review, StoryQuarterly, Southwest Review* and elsewhere; his stage play, *Arborophilia*, premiered at the Detroit Repertory Theater. Jacob can be found on the internet at www.jacobmappel.com.

David Appelbaum is an inveterate biker and is the publisher of Codhill Press.

Annecy Baez is a poet and short story writer. Her most recent literary work, *The Red Shoes*, was translated by Ruth Herrera and appeared in Spanish as *Tacones Rojos* in *Caudal*, a literary journal in the Dominican Republic. Other work has appeared in *Tertuliand/Hanging Out*, a bilingual literary anthology published by Hunter Caribbean Studies, and *Callaloo*, an African American Literary Journal from John Hopkins University. She lives with her supportive husband and daughter in Irvington On Hudson.

Jerrice Baptiste was born in Haiti. She earned a Masters Degree in Education, and has studied Poetry Therapy. Jerrice currently facilitates poetry workshops in the Hudson Valley. She is the founder of AuthenticPoetry.com and also the host of "Women of Note" on 98.1FM WKZE. Her poetry has been published in *African Voices, Human Journey Magazine, Nubian Poets, Events Quarterly* and many others.

William Boyle was born and raised in Brooklyn, lived in the Hudson Valley for ten years, and now resides in the Bronx. He has published short stories, poems, and essays in *The Shawangunk Review, Aethlon, Prima Materia, Out of the Gutter*, and several other journals and magazines. He has also recently completed work on a novel, *The Gravesend Kid*.

Laurence Carr writes drama, fiction and poetry. Over 30 plays and theatre pieces have been produced in NYC, regionally and in Europe, including *Vaudeville, 36 Exposures, The Voyage of Mary C. and The American Auditions*. Numerous poems have been published and his book of microfiction, *The Wytheport Tales*, is published by Codhill Press. He teaches Dramatic and Creative Writing at SUNY New Paltz.

Lucia Cherciu was born in Romania. She is an Assistant Professor of English at Dutchess Community College, Poughkeepsie, NY. Her previous publications include an essay, "A Veritable Guest to Her Own Self: Mary Wilkins Freeman's Humorous Short Stories," published in *The Journal of the Short Story in English*; an essay, "Parody as Dialogue and Disenchantment: Remembering Phoebe Cary," published in *American Transcendental Quarterly*; and "Woman and the Land in the Romanian Agrarian Novel," which appeared as a chapter in *The Literature of Nature: An International Handbook*.

Samuel Claiborne is a poet, essayist, composer, musician and photographer originally from New York City, now based in the Hudson Valley. His work has been published in *Northern Light, Halfmoon Review, Belle Fourche, Chronogram* and most recently, *Vanguard Voic-*

es of the Hudson Valley – Poetry 2007. He is currently at work on his first novel, *NODding Out,* and has just released a CD of solo acoustic piano improvisations, *The Annunciation*, on Sonotrope Recordings.

Suzanne Cleary's poetry books are *Trick Pear* (2007) and *Keeping Time* (2002), both published by Carnegie Mellon University Press. Her awards include a Pushcart Prize and the Cecil Hemley Memorial Award of the Poetry Society of America. She is co-editor of Slapering Hol Press, of the Hudson Valley Writers' Center, and Professor of English at SUNY Rockland.

Brenda Connor-Bey is the Poet Laureate for the Town of Greenburgh, NY. She is the author of *Thoughts of an Everyday Woman/An Unfinished Urban Folktale*, a member of the Advisory Committees for the Slapering Hol Press, the Westchester Center for Creative Aging; and a member of the Poetry Caravan. A recipient of the Westchester Fund for Women and Girls' Outstanding Arts Educator Award, a NYS CAPS award for poetry, four PEN awards for non-fiction and a NYFA for fiction, Brenda is a MacDowell, YADDO and Cave Canem Regional Fellow.

Teresa Marta Costa is a resident of West Hurley, NY. She currently hosts two poetry readings in Kingston at The Bohemian Book Bin and The Muddy Cup. She is listed in The American Poets & Writers Directory. Her chapbooks include *Cosmic Orgasm* (manxcat press) and *Gone Fishing*.

James Finn Cotter is a professor of English at Mount Saint Mary College, Newburgh NY. He is the author of *Inscape: The Christology and Poetry of Gerard Manley Hopkins* and of articles on Dante, Chaucer, Sidney, Hopkins and Salinger. He has translated *The Divine Comedy*, published by SUNY Stony Brook. He is president of the International Hopkins Association. His poetry has been published in *America, The Commonweal, The Hudson Review, The Nation, The*

New York Times, Sparrow, Spirit, Thought, and other periodicals. He is also the author of *Beginnings: the first Twenty-Five Years of Mount Saint Mary College*.

Laura Shaine Cunningham is a playwright and journalist whose fiction and nonfiction have appeared in *The New Yorker, The Atlantic Monthly, The New York Times, Vogue, Harper's Bazaar*, and other publications. The recipient of numerous awards and fellowships for her writing and theatrical work, Cunningham divides her time between New York City and her place in the country.

Da Chen is the acclaimed bestselling author of *Colors of the Mountain*, which was a New England Booksellers Association Discovery Selection, a Book Sense 76 Selection, a Borders Original Voices Selection, and a Barnes and Noble Discover Great New Writers Selection. His young adult autobiography, *China's Son*, was a Borders Original Voices Award finalist, an American Library Association Best Books for Young Adults final nominee, a New York Public Library Book for the Teen Age, and a PBS TeacherSource recommended book. His newest novel, *Brothers*, has recently been nominated for a 2007 Quill Award in general fiction. www.dachen.org

Enid Dame (1943-2003) published seven books of poetry, an anthology of writings on Lilith, and numerous poems, short stories, reviews, and essays in periodicals. She co-edited both the literary tabloid *Home Planet News* and the Jewish feminist journal, *Bridges*, and taught literature and creative writing at Rutgers, NJIT, and other institutions. She received many awards for her writing.

Lynne Digby's visual art is included in the McGraw-Hill collection. A solo show at the Woodstock Artists Association & Museum is entitled "Magnificent Maine in Mixed Media". Her book of illustrated poems, from which *Farewell to Summer* is taken, is entitled *May I share with you?,* which she also illustrated. She is a co-founder of the

Warwick Valley Writers Group. Her fantasy, *Simeon & the Witches of Tarrascon*, tells how a little cat, unknowingly, through unconditional love saves the planet of Tarrascon.

Dennis Doherty is Coordinator of Creative Writing and chair of the Poetry Board at SUNY New Paltz, where he teaches creative writing and literature. Poems in this anthology appear in his collection *The Bad Man* (Ye Olde Font Shoppe Press) and the forthcoming *Fugitive* (Codhill Press). "Designs" won second prize in the national Robert Frost Foundation competition.

Alec Emerson, having always been a bookworm, has enjoyed writing since junior high school (for a teacher named Socrates). He started writing again in 1988 when he attended Harvard. In 2000, he decided to write for ten years.

Staats Fasoldt is an artist who teaches painting at The Woodstock School of Art. He moved to Ulster County from Albany, in 1976, to attend the MFA program at SUNY New Paltz, and fell in love with the area. "I began trying to write poetry after reading Jack Karouac, whose language seemed alive to me."

Allen C. Fischer, former director of marketing for a corporation, brings to poetry a background in business. His poems have been published in *Atlanta Review, Indiana Review, The Laurel Review, Poetry, Prairie Schooner, Rattle* and *River Styx*.

Howard Good, a journalism professor at SUNY New Paltz, is the author of two poetry chapbooks, *Death of the Frog Prince* (2004) and *Heartland* (2007), both from FootHills Publishing. His poems have appeared in numerous print and online journals, including *Right Hand Pointing, Stirring, Flutter, Inscribed, Why Vandalism?, Raving Dove, New Verse News, Eclectica, Persistent Image, Mad Swirl, The Flask Review, The Rose & Thorn, Juked, The Orange Room Review*, and *Lily*. He was nominated for a Pushcart Prize in 2006.

Author Biographies

Anne Gorrick's work has appeared in: *American Letters and Commentary, the Cortland Review, Fence, Gutcult, Hunger Magazine, MiPOesias, No Tell Motel, the Seneca Review, Sulfur* and *word for/ word*. Collaborating with artist Cynthia Winika, she produced a limited edition artists' book called *"Swans, the ice," she said* through the Women's Studio Workshop in Rosendale, NY. In addition to being a bookmaker, she also works in encaustic, printmaking and traditional Japanese papermaking. She lives in West Park, New York and curates the poetry series "Cadmium Text."

Sari Grandstaff lives in the Hudson Valley with her husband and three children. Her work is heard on several Northeast Public Radio Programs and has been published in MiPoesias, Sierra Nevada College Review, Nthposition, Home Planet News, Red River Review, Jerseyworks, Mom Writers Literary Magazine and Modern Haiku among others.

Carol Graser hosts a monthly poetry series at Saratoga Spring's historic Caffe Lena and has performed her work at various events and venues around NYS. Her work has been published in many literary journals including *Chaffin, artisan, Berkeley Poetry Review* and *Big Hammer*. Her book, *The Wild Twist of Their Stems*, will be published by Foothills Publishing.

Eamon Grennan's recent books of poetry are *Still Life With Waterfall* and *The Quick Of It*. His forthcoming volume, *Matter Of Fact*, (two poems from it appear in this volume), will be out in Spring 2008 from Graywolf. He has taught at Vassar College for many years, and currently teaches in the graduate writing programs of NYU and Columbia. His translation (with Rachel Kitzinger) of Sophocles's *Oedipus At Colonus* appeared recently from Oxford.

Don Haynie is a songwriter and singer best known for his work in the duo Haynie & Samuel. With four albums of his songs to their credit (and a fifth due out soon), they have toured the U.S. an almost uncountable number of times, and been heard around the world, thanks to the magic of radio.

Werner Hengst grew up in Germany during WWII, emigrated to the US in 1953. He is the co-founder of Our Montessori School, a private school serving about 300 children. Currently, he is working on a collection of memoirs and personal essays. His work has appeared in *Snowy Egret, Smithsonian, Prima Materia, Mohican* and elsewhere.

Mala Hoffman is a poet and freelance journalist whose work has been showcased in a variety of publications, including *Chronogram, The Village Voice* and *The River Reporter*. She lives in Gardiner, New York with her husband Marc Moran and daughters Lucy and Sadie. Her poetry collection, *Half Moon Over Midnight*, was published by Paper Kite Press in December 2006.

Mikhail Horowitz is the author of *Big League Poets* (City Lights), *The Opus of Everything in Nothing Flat* (Red Hill), and *Rafting Into the Afterlife* (Codhill Press). His performance work has been featured on a dozen CDs, including *The Blues of the Birth* (Sundazed Records). Since 2001 he has toiled as an impecunious redactor in the Bard College Publications Office.

Kate Hymes is a poet and educator living in New Paltz, New York. She has been a featured reader at many local venues. Her poems have been published in journals and anthologies, most recently the Cave Canem 10 Year Anniversary Anthology, *Gathering Ground*, (University of Michigan Press). Kate leads writing workshops in New Paltz and co-leads the workshop "If We Are Sisters: Black and White Women Write Across Race" with Pat Schneider, Director Emeritus of Amherst Writers and Artists. www.wallkillvalleywriters.com.

Heinz Insu Fenkl teaches Creative Writing at SUNY New Paltz. His new book is a translation of older Korean verse. His acclaimed memoir of growing up in cold-war Korea, *Memories of my Ghost Brother*, was published in 1996.

Mike Jurkovic's poems have appeared in *The South Carolina Review, The Comstock Review, Confluence, The Baltimore Review, RiverSedge, Main Street Rag, Meridian Anthology, The Haight Ashbury Literary Review, Heaven Bone, Diner, Home Planet News*, and *The Wisconsin Review Anthologies Will Work For Peace* (Zeropanik,1999), *Dyed-In-The-Wool: A Hudson River Poetry Anthology* (Vivisphere, 2001). Co-director of the Calling All Poets Reading Series, Beacon, NY & host of the annual Hudson Valley Poets Fest. CD reviews appear regularly in *Chronogram* and *The Folk and Acoustic Music Exchange*. His column, "The Rock 'n Roll Curmudgeon", appeared in *Rhythm and News Magazine 1997-2004*.

Christine Boyka Kluge is the author of *Teaching Bones to Fly* (2003) and *Stirring the Mirror* (2007), both from Bitter Oleander Press. Her chapbook, *Domestic Weather* (2004), won the 2003 Uccelli Press Chapbook Contest. Other honors include winning the 2006 Hotel Amerika Poetry Contest and the 1999 Frances Locke Memorial Poetry Award, and receiving several Pushcart Prize nominations.

C.J. Krieger is a poet, singer, songwriter and massage therapist. His music and writings have been recorded and in print since the late 1960's. He has been published in the *The Poetry Review* and has written three books: *Pinacolada Child, There's Always August*, and *Absorbed by the Sun*. His newest book: *Reflections In Glass*, will be published Nov/Dec of this year. CJ is in love with the Catskills!

Frank LaRonca's poems have appeared in *Chronogram, RATTLE* and most recently as a "notable" selection for this year's *Vanguard Voices of the Hudson Valley – Poetry 2007*. A middle school special education teacher, Frank lives in idyllic New Paltz with his wife and two young daughters.

AUTHOR BIOGRAPHIES

Robert Leaver is a NYC/West Shokan based teacher, artist and writer whose work spans a variety of mediums. He has written for national magazines, local newspapers, film, television and lyrics for his band, Raw Believer.

Sharmagne Leland-St. John, a Native American poet, concert performer, lyricist, artist, and film-maker is the Editor-in-Chief of the poetry e-zine "Quill and Parchment.com." She has published three poetry collections, *Unsung Songs, Silver Tears and Time, Contingencies*, and co-authored a book on film production design, *Designing Movies: Portrait of a Hollywood Artist*.

Donald Lev lives in High Falls, NY where he edits and publishes *Home Planet News*, the arts tabloid he and his late wife Enid Dame founded in 1979. His poetry has been widely published in periodicals and anthologies and there have been fourteen collections of his poetry published since 1968.

Phillip Levine lives on the side of a mountain and struggles daily to keep from slipping off. He juggles that with being a dad, poetry editor for *Chronogram* magazine and host of the weekly Monday night reading series and open-mike at the Colony Cafe in Woodstock, NY, among a number of other balls and boulders.

Nadine Lewis is a Hudson Valley visual artist and poet. She has written several chapbooks including *Damning the Muse!* and *Between Belly and Womb* and edited *Core Pieces* and *Literary Passions*, among others.

Steven Lewis is a Mentor at Empire State College and a freelance writer. Recent books are *Zen and the Art of Fatherhood, The ABCs of Real Family Values* and *The Complete Guide for the Anxious Groom*. *Fear and Loathing of Boca Raton: A Hippies' Guide to the Second Sixties* and *A Month on a Barrier Island* (poetry) are forthcoming.

Brian Liston is a poet and short-story writer who hopes that his contribution will inspire people who have mental disorders that they can achieve anything if they set their minds to it. Features include Cross Street Altieir in Saugerties, Cubbie Hole in Poughkeepsie and The Colony Café in Woodstock and have been included in such magazines as *Chronogram*, the *Post Star* and *The Awakening*.

Valerie Martin was born in Sedalia, Missouri, and grew up in New Orleans, Louisiana, where her father was a sea-captain. She is the author of seven novels, including *Mary Reilly, The Great Divorce, Italian Fever*, and *Property*, three collections of short fiction, and a biography of St. Francis of Assisi, titled *Salvation*. She has been awarded a grant from the National Endowment for the Arts, as well as the Kafka Prize (for *Mary Reilly*) and Britain's Orange Prize (for *Property*). A new novel, *Trespass* will be published by Nan A. Talese in September of 2007. Valerie Martin has taught in writing programs at Mt. Holyoke College, Univ. of Massachusetts, and Sarah Lawrence College, among others. She resides in upstate New York

Robert Milby, of Florida, NY has shared his work in the Hudson Valley and beyond, since 1995. He's published in *Home Planet News, Hunger Magazine, Will Work For Peace*, and others. CD: *Revenant Echo* (Sonotrope Recordings, 2004). His first book was *Ophelia's Offspring* (Foothills Publishing, June, 2007). He writes for *The Delaware and Hudson Canvas*, in Bloomingburgh, NY, and hosts local poetry readings. www.robertmilby.com

Karen Neuberg is a poet living and writing in West Hurley, NY and Brooklyn. Her work has appeared in literature journals such as *Barrow Street, Columbia Poetry Review, Diner, and Phoebe*, and on-line for *Shampoo, The Diagram, Toasted-Cheese, Caffeine Destiny, Free Verse*, and others. She is a Pushcart nominee and holds an MFA from The New School.

Author Biographies

Will Nixon has published two chapbooks, *When I Had It Made* (Pudding House), and *The Fish Are Laughing* (Pavement Saw). He has completed a cyberpunk epic, *Lyndon Baines Takes a Fare to the Palace of Wisdom*, and a chapbook inspired by the movie, *Night of the Living Dead*. He lives in Woodstock, NY.

James P. Othmer is the author of the novel *The Futurist*. His stories and essays have appeared in numerous publications. This story is from a novel in progress. He can be reached at www.jamespothmer.com.

Jo Pitkin holds an M.F.A. from the University of Iowa. Her poems have appeared in *Ironwood, Quarterly West, Nimrod*, and other magazines, and Finishing Line Press published her chapbook, *The Measure*. In 2007, she won Third Prize in Mohonk Mountain Stage Company's regional contest, Vanguard Voices of the Hudson Valley, as well as Third Prize in the Connecticut River Review Poetry Contest.

Robert Polito lives in New Paltz and New York City, where he directs the Graduate Writing Program at the New School. His many books include *Doubles* (Chicago), *A Reader's Guide to James Merrill's The Changing Light at Sandover* (Michigan), and *Savage Art: A Biography of Jim Thompson* (Knopf/Vintage) which received the National Book Critics Circle Award in biography. He recently edited *The Selected Poems of Kenneth Fearing* for the Library of America, and his essay "Shame" appeared in *Best American Essays 2006*. His next book of poems is tentatively titled *Hollywood & God*, and he is editing *The Complete Film Writings of Manny Farber*.

Gretchen Primack's publication credits include *The Paris Review, Prairie Schooner, FIELD, New Orleans Review, Rhino, Best New Poets 2006*, and others. Her chapbook, *Space and a Bird*, is forthcoming from Finishing Line Press, while her full-length manuscript, *Fiery Cake*, has been shortlisted for several prizes. She lives in Hurley with a beloved human and several beloved rescued animals. She serves on the board of Catskill Animal Sanctuary and teaches at SUNY-Ulster, Bard College, and two prisons through the Bard Prison Initiative.

Guy Reed has published essays in the *Saugerties Times*, the online arts journal *Mental Contagion*, and in the anthologies *Prima Materia Vol. 3*, *My Heart's First Steps: Writings That Celebrate The Gifts of Parenthood*, and *Resistant Tongues: Mid-Hudson Valley Poets Against The War*. He lives in the Catskill Mountains with his wife and their two children.

Marilyn Reynolds has worked throughout her life as a writer but primarily as a visual artist. She gave her first reading of her prose and poetry in 2005 in the Hudson Opera House alongside a major exhibition of her paintings and drawings. She recently completed *Paper Thin, a memoir, ring I*.

Cheryl A. Rice, a Long Islander by birth, has made the Hudson Valley home for twenty-seven years. Founder of the 'Sylvia Plath Bake-Off', a combination open mic/baked goods contest, her poems have appeared in *Bitterroot, Chronogram, The Florida Review, Home Planet News, Mangrove, Other: -----, The Temple/El Templo*, and *The Woodstock Times*. http://www.geocities.com/dorothyy62/flyingmonkeyproductions.html.

Tad Richards' recent poetry publications include *Cortland Review, Phoebe (The George Mason Review), Iowa Review, Fragments* (UK) and *Fieralingue Poets Corner* (Italy). Two poetry collections, *Situations* and *My Night With the Language Thieves*, have been published by Ye Olde Font Shoppe Press, which will issue a new chapbook, *Take Five: Poems in 5/4 Time*, this year.

R. E. Rigolino grew up in The Bronx before attending Vassar College and later SUNY New Paltz. She currently teaches first-year Composition at SUNY New Paltz and lives in Highland with her husband and two sons. A writer of fiction, Rigolino won first place in the *Poughkeepsie Journal's* "Talespinners" competition in 2004 for her short story, *The Hunt*.

Abigail Robin is a writer, teacher, actor, director, and producer. Now residing in Kingston, she moved to Woodstock before the 1969 Woodstock Festival, built a house and made dinner for Sarah and Bob Dylan. She created ART- Abigail Robin Tours, artist studio tours in the Hudson Valley and NYC. She recently co-produced and performed in Howard Zinn's play, *Emma*, about activist Emma Goldman at Woodstock's Byrdcliffe Theatre. A memoir, *L'Chaim*, has recently been published. She teaches at SUNY New Paltz.

Anthony Robinson, Professor (emeritus) of English at SUNY New Paltz and Director of the Creative Writing Program for twenty years, is the author of five novels. He has just finished a new novel called *The American Golfer*. Mr. Robinson, who holds a BA and MA degree from Columbia, lives with his wife Tania on Huguenot Street in New Paltz.

Kenneth Salzmann's poems have appeared in *Rattle, The Peninsula Review, The Comstock Review, Medicinal Purposes, Spillway, The Piedmont Literary Review, The Sow's Ear Poetry Review, California Quarterly, Chronogram* and elsewhere. He lives in Woodstock and Troy, New York. Formerly vice president of The Arts Center of the Capital Region in Troy, New York, he is now associated with Gelles-Cole Literary Enterprises, an editorial boutique serving authors, publishers and agents. He is a member of the Woodstock Poetry Society.

Judith Saunders teaches at Marist College. Her poems have been published in *Chronogram, Oxalis, The Hudson Valley Review, Poet Magazine*, and *Thelma*, among others.

Author Biographies

Jan Zlotnik Schmidt is a SUNY Distinguished Teaching Professor in the Department of English at SUNY New Paltz. Her poetry has been published in *Kansas Quarterly, Cream City Review, Syracuse Scholar, Alaska Quarterly Review, Home Planet News*, and *Phoebe*. She has published two volumes of poetry—*We Speak in Tongues* (the Edwin Mellen Press, 1991) and *She had this memory* (The Edwin Mellen Press 2000), and two collections of autobiographical essays—*Women/Writing/Teaching* (SUNY Press 1998) and *Wise Women: Reflections of Teachers at Midlife*, co-authored with Dr. Phyllis R. Freeman (Routledge 2000).

William Seaton is an *homme des lettres*: poet, scholar, critic and translator. His work appeared in such journals as *Chelsea, Mad Blood, Home Planet News*, and *Heaven Bone*, as well as in the chapbook, *Tourist Snapshots*. He has been active in poetry performance since the 1960s and currently produces the "Poetry On the Loose" series.

Nina Shengold's first novel, *Clearcut*, was published by Anchor Books in 2005. She won the Writers Guild Award for her teleplay, *Labor of Love*, and the ABC Playwright Award for *Homesteaders*. She has edited twelve theatre anthologies for Vintage and Viking Penguin, and is Books Editor of *Chronogram* magazine. She lives in The Vly.

Sparrow lives by the Esopus River, in Phoenicia, New York. He is gossip columnist for the *Phoenicia Times*. Sparrow's most recent book is *America: A Prophecy -- The Sparrow Reader* (Soft Skull Press). He is learning to play the "mountain harmonica."

Matthew J. Spireng of Lomontville won the 2004 Bluestem Poetry Award for his book, *Out of Body*, published in 2006 by Bluestem Press at Emporia State University. His chapbooks are: *Young Farmer*, 2007; *Encounters*, 2005; *Just This*, 2003; and *Inspiration Point*, winner of the 2000 Bright Hill Press Poetry Chapbook Competition, 2002. His poems have appeared widely since 1990.

AUTHOR BIOGRAPHIES

Margo Stever's *Frozen Spring* won the 2002 Mid-List Press First Series Award for Poetry. Her chapbook, *Reading the Night Sky*, won the 1996 Riverstone Press Chapbook Competition. Her poems have appeared in the *Seattle Review, West Branch, Connecticut Review, Rattapallax*, and elsewhere. She is the founding editor of the Slapering Hol Press and founder of The Hudson Valley Writers' Center.

H.R. Stoneback is a Distinguished Professor of English at SUNY New Paltz. He is a Hemingway scholar of international reputation, author/editor of twelve books and over 100 essays on Durrell, Faulkner, Hemingway, et al. He is a widely published poet, author of five volumes, including *Café Millenium* and *Homage: A Letter to Robert Penn Warren*. His book, *Reading Hemingway's The Sun Also Rises*, is the inaugural volume in the "Reading Hemingway Series" from Kent State University Press.

Christine Lilian Turczyn is a poet and educator, who has taught at Dutchess Community College and William Paterson University. Her awards include first prize in the Allen Ginsberg poetry awards, an Associated Writing Programs' Intro Award, an award from the Academy of American Poets and honorable mention in the Rita Dove National Poetry. She was awarded first prize in the Mohonk Mountain Stage Company's *Vanguard Voices of the Hudson Valley – Poetry 2007* competition. Her second collection of poems is *The Sky Inside Your Body*. Her work has appeared numerous publications.

Pauline Uchmanowicz is the author of the chapbook *Sand & Traffic* (Codhill Press, 2004). Her poems and essays have appeared in numerous publications, including *Ploughshares, Crazyhorse, Ohio Review, Southern Poetry Review, The Massachusetts Review*, and *Z Magazine*. She is a food columnist for *Woodstock Times* (New York) and frequent contributor to the arts-and-culture magazine *Chronogram*.

Author Biographies

Robert H. Waugh is a Professor of English at SUNY New Paltz and the Director of the annual Lovecraft Forum. He is the author of *The Monster in the Mirror: Looking for H.P. Lovecraft* and many articles on science fiction, horror and fantasy literature, which have been published in such journals as *Extrapolation* and *Lovecraft Studies*. He is also a widely published poet; his chapbook, *Shorewards, Tidewards*, is published by Codhill Press.

Bruce Weber is the author of four published books of poetry, most recently *Poetic Justice* (Icon Press, 2004). His group, The No Chance Ensemble, has produced the CD *Let's Dine Like Jack Johnson Tonight*. He is also the producer of the 13-years-running Alternative New Year's Day Spoken Word/Performance Extravaganza in New York City.

Nancy Willard was born in Ann Arbor, Michigan. She was educated at the University of Michigan and Stanford University. Willard is the author of twelve books of poetry, including *Water Walker*, which was nominated for the National Book Critics Circle Award, and *In the Salt Marsh*. She has also written two novels, and four books of stories and essays. She lives in New York and teaches at Vassar College in Poughkeepsie, NY.

Bob Wright, who currently resides in Athens, New York, is the host of a bimonthly poetry reading at the Athens Cultural Center and is the curator of the web-based Hudson Valley Poetry Calendar (www.poetz.com/hudson), a comprehensive listing of poetry events in the counties along the Hudson River. He has read throughout the Northeast and been published in such diverse periodicals as *Oxalis, Yankee, the Christian Science Monitor, Freefall Magazine, Heliotrope*, and *The North Dakota Quarterly*.

Sarah Wyman, self-schooled in writing her way into the world, finally studied creative writing at Hollins University in Roanoke, VA. She now works as an Assistant Professor of English at SUNY New Paltz. Before joining the New Paltz faculty, she taught at the University of North Carolina at Chapel Hill, and in Konstanz, Germany. Her scholarship and teaching involve twentieth-century US literature, women's writing, and studies in Word & Image, particularly poetry and painting as parallel semiotic systems.